THE ART OF MAGICK

The Mystery of Deep Magick & Divine Rituals

Gabriyell Sarom

Contents

Publications

  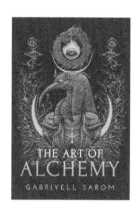

The Art of Mysticism

Practical Guide to Mysticism & Spiritual Meditations

The Art of Occultism

The Secrets of High Occultism & Inner Exploration

The Art of Alchemy

Inner Alchemy & the Revelation of the Philosopher's Stone

Subscribe to Gabriyell Sarom's Newsletter and receive the book:

Divine Abilities: 3 Techniques to Awaken Divine Abilities

www.sacredmystery.org

Introduction

For thousands of years, mankind has been practicing magick under different denominations, traditions, and systems. However, in today's world, magick seems to have been left behind, collecting dirt, buried in the dark corners of human history. This is no surprise. Fear, dogma, and disreputable arcane teachings appear to have assaulted it. But this is not authentic magick.

Real magick is a beautiful system that stood untouched throughout the ages. It is a mystifying expedition into the exotic realms of the unknown, manifesting profound change within and without. Now, it's time to illuminate it anew, leaving all of these lightless tenets behind once and for all.

The magick presented in this book is vehemently pragmatic, unique, and innovative. It is not the customary approach of regurgitating magickal traditionalism. Many of the techniques taught in those obscure books are packed with chaff to conceal the real essence of the methods. Don't expect to find that same approach and teachings here. This work doesn't tackle superficial magick, but magick for profound self-transformation and self-transcendence. It also provides the reader with the necessary tools to create their own practices and rituals.

Furthermore, it expounds the forgotten teachings of Deep Magick. Expect disruption, and see it as part of the unfolding process that magick infuses into life. Once the power of magick is tasted, life will never be seen in the same way again. Instead of being passive co-creators of this awe-inspiring Creation, we become active painters of beautiful universal art.

At various points in history, there has been a master, a book, or a teaching that inspires adepts to embark on a magickal journey of self-experimentation. We sincerely hope the reader enjoys this work and that it may serve as that impetus of inspiration that reveals the timeless art of magick.

SECTION 1
The Baptism

1

What is Magick?

All human beings have an innate power in themselves. Many have never heard about that power, but they can feel it. We all feel something inside, something special that we can't fully understand. Magick is a tool that helps us tap into that power and use it to improve ourselves, our life, and our spiritual and mystical path. It is the art of creating change in accordance to our will.

Most people think that magick is some ridiculous and evil doctrine, propagated by uneducated, doctrinaire, or destructive people. This is because, throughout centuries, magick has been misused and degraded into arcane sorcery, superficial rituals, and nefarious practices such as sacrificing live chickens.

Regardless of what many people claim or think, magick isn't evil or destructive, just like a knife isn't evil. It all depends on its use. Anything can be corrupted or misused.

Furthermore, the belief that performing magick is something laughable and bizarre is foolish. Mindlessly eating highly-processed food, sitting every day behind a screen in a cubicle for over 40 years, and living a totally sedentary life immersed in ignorance is what's bizarre, harmful, and laughable. Anyone who studies authentic magick discovers that sewing frogs' mouths is not part of the list of teachings.

Magick actually has an inherent luminosity, and is more than an assemblage of mysterious principles and esoteric theories. It is a concrete tradition with procedures that are designed to produce a powerful shift in the student's mind, body, and soul.

The highest use of magick is to harmonize ourselves with the universe and God. It's what multiple traditions and mystical disciplines allude to when they teach about accomplishing enlightenment or finding the "Kingdom of Heaven" within.

Magick is a perennial journey of divine beauty, and no one in this world will ever unfold it in its entirety. But everyone can take part in this mysterious adventure. Those who study and practice magick their whole lives will evolve as multidimensional beings, reaching unforeseeable heights.

Ultimately, magick is about improving and transcending our human experience. We conquer and expand our limits, blooming into our innate divinity. That's what real magick is all about.

2

The Pantheon of Oneness

agick is not a modern or new subject. Before all religions came into being, magick was already present. To help the student understand how deep it goes, we shall give a brief description of its ancient origins.

With the rise of the first nomadic tribes, the first magicians also appeared. Called shamans, these men had a strong bond with the forces of nature, and their main job was to cause rain, dissipate clouds, keep diseases at bay, and help to find food and water. Some spiritual researchers affirm that the early primitive paintings of these tribes not only showed the achievements of their hunts but were also magickal works to attract success in new hunts.

Shamans played a prominent role because they mediated

the relationship between the physical world and the subtle worlds to ensure the survival of their tribes, often utilizing the personification and anthropomorphization of the natural forces and energies ("gods") as a means of performing their magick and rituals.

Later, as tribes began to settle and implement agriculture, they also began to organize and structure into small civilizations. At this point, shamans progressively became the known class of "priests", turning their personified gods into a systemized and mystical pantheon. This phenomenon can be seen all over the world in the most varied cultures, from Hinduism to Hermeticism. Nowadays, due to multiple distortions or modifications, all of these cultures that stood the test of time have autonomous religious, spiritual, or mystical systems, and they may even have completely different teachings and philosophies. Each religion or mystical tradition has its own representation (i.e., "gods"), though some may be quite similar (Zeus and Jupiter; Ra and Surya; etc.) because after all, they actually came from the same source.

When practicing magick, a pantheon can be useful because it helps our minds connect with the forces that a specific god represents, which could otherwise be considered abstract and untouchable. On the contrary, it can also become an obstacle, if we begin to worship those idols and their forms, instead of seeing them for the purpose they originally had. Additionally, today's culture has mostly been disconnected from these ancient gods and figures. Consequently, our suggestion is more in the direction of using universal symbols than personified forces. But each student should choose according to their inclinations.

Despite what many people may assume, these ancient cultures were not fools. Though some people back then may have believed that these gods were entities that literally existed, real magick practitioners knew that they were actually invoking, evoking, connecting, or engaging with the energy of that specific force (e.g., visualizing, meditating, or praying to Ra is a symbolic method of engaging with the subtle mystical energy of the Sun, related to the vital force).

It is critical to comprehend that despite having countless gods for every type of force, energy, or even state, many traditions also highlight the oneness of God. God is just One, not many. God is the primordial substance, the source, Spirit, or the underlying foundation of all that is. Because of God's inconceivable, unthinkable, and unknowable nature, we imaginarily "split" Him into different aspects to get to know Him to the best of our ability.

All truthful magickal traditions know that even though a polytheistic system can be useful, God is only one. This is a critical principle, one that a student of magick must never forget, otherwise they may become trapped into an unending loop of seeking illusions. Implementing this fundamental knowledge into your magickal practices is what will ultimately help you to pursue the supreme and transcend into your divine form. That's what many magick books end up overlooking, but that's also why you're reading this one. There are no coincidences.

3

Is Magick Worth Your Time?

agick is not an easy discipline. It requires a lot of energy, continuous practice, relentless effort, self-control, and mighty willpower.

Nevertheless, the reader is already performing a form of magick, regardless if they are aware of it or not. Whenever someone has a thought that gives rise to an intention that leads them to perform an action that ends up influencing their life or the world, they are doing a form of magick. However, they may do this unconsciously, which could potentially bring negative consequences, such as when someone has a negative thought about something that has the effect of making them perform an action that will not bring positive results.

The difference between this and actual magick is that in the latter, the magick practitioner is taking full control of this process, enabling them to intentionally wield influence on reality. This will speed up their evolution and mystical path, limited only by their beliefs and by how much of their life the practitioner devotes to magick. One thing is guaranteed: if a student practices magick correctly, their life will never be the same.

Several disciplines have been developed to help human beings enhance the quality of their lives, control their minds, and transcend their limitations. Buddhism, Yoga, Zen, Hermeticism, Kabbalah, and Occultism are some of them. Magick also belongs to this category, though many mystic traditions already incorporate some degree of magick into their systems.

Through the methods employed in magick, such as concentration, visualization, or subconscious self-hypnosis, we can improve our self and alter external conditions. This occurs due to the intimate connection between our inner world (microcosm) and outer world (macrocosm).

Beyond the ancient exploration of new lands, and the recent yet still infant space exploration, the exploration of the inner dimension is the most extraordinary and breathtaking subject in the human realm.

Magick is a mysterious journey into the unknown. It will always be fascinating and intriguing, and whether the reader dives into it in this lifetime or another, it will always be there with its secrets, awaiting to be experienced by those who authentically pursue the limits of the human condition.

4

Magick vs. Magic

We all know what *magic* is: tricks and illusions. In magic, there are stage performances where the magician levitates half-clothed assistants, pulls rabbits out of hats, and performs impossible feats before a live audience. It is entertainment.

Magick, on the other hand, with a "k", is a mystical and spiritual discipline. It is a combination of multiple spiritual traditions from both the East and West, containing mind-altering wisdom and potent meditative and ritualistic practices.

Fundamentally, magic consists of deceiving others through tricks, leading them to believe, for a moment, that the impossible is possible. It is the art of illusion. The successful magician (illusionist) never reveals their tricks, and the more exuberant and bigger the show, the better.

Contrarily, magick at its core is a continuous process of discovering and understanding the multidimensional universe that we live in, an odyssey of self-transcendence that leads us to shape our own reality. It's not related to tricks or shows, but to methods of using our mental and energetic abilities to pierce through the physical barriers into subtler dimensions of existence. With the conscious engagement with these subtler levels of reality, we can alter the unconscious roots of our psyche, and even modify the physical level of reality according to certain rules, laws, and in compliance with our karma.

There's really no comparison between both. One deceives, while the other illuminates. Nonetheless, even within magick, we can unfold it into two modalities:

- *Regular Magick*, which concentrates mostly on mundane desires and urges, and on fulfilling less divine goals. Some magicians disapprove of using magick for such needs, because they see it as being superficial, greedy, earthly-minded, and focused on the self. We shouldn't see it as wrong or less noble, but just less mystical and divine.

It may be hard to discover the mysteries of reality or uniting with God when worries concerning your physical needs (health, food, security, etc.) are constantly floating in the mind. After all, being healthy and having money doesn't make any-one less sacred or divine. If a student possesses a strong and healthy body and mind, they will have fewer obstacles in their mystical and spiritual path. If a student possesses financial stability, they don't have to worry much about fulfilling their basic survival needs and those of their family. There's really nothing wrong with this type of magick.

- *Deep Magick*, which is essentially about mystical and spiritual growth.

This is the type of magick that we will mainly address in this book. Deep Magick helps us not only change the core of our psyche into something greater and more divine but also shape the very reality we live in. We can use it as a way to decipher universal wisdom, experience magickal states, and as a path towards union with God. It is a tremendously powerful system of evolution and transcendence.

Magick, with a "k" doesn't pretend to make the impossible possible. It really does it.

5

As Above, So Below

As above, so below, as within, so without, as the universe, so the soul.

— Hermes Trismegistus

ll dimensions or planes of existence are intrinsically linked in the same way fire, heat, and smoke are. Anything that we do one plane affects the other. For example, if a student has a negative thought (mental plane), that thought can give birth to a negative emotion (energetic plane), which may tense the student's body (physical plane).

There are situations in which a change in a grosser plane can temporarily alter a subtler plane (e.g., performing exercise may release endorphins which causes the mind to relax), but for the most part, it's altering something in the subtler planes that triggers changes in the lower and grosser planes. Nonetheless, each plane of reality, to a greater or lesser extent, has the power to affect others.

Typically, thoughts generate energy and emotions, giving even more power and attention towards those original thoughts, solidifying them, and climaxing in their manifestation in the physical plane. This is also how magick works. The difference, however, is that instead of letting unconscious patterns and thoughts alter the grosser dimensions of reality, practitioners of magick consciously employ the mind and will to perform this process.

They know that reality is not only made out of matter, and that there are other subtler dimensions of reality, many of which we consciously interact with every day, such as thoughts, emotions, and energy. They are the pragmatic scientists of the mystical arts, living their multidimensional lives to their fullest.

Evidently, with great power and wisdom comes great responsibility. Some practitioners take this knowledge for their own benefit while purposely spreading harm and affecting others. But the universe has a way of balancing things out, so we caution those who, instead of using magick to improve themselves, their lives, and their mystical path, may be thinking of using magick to attack others, disrupt lives, or worse.

Ultimately, the profundity of Hermes' remarkable affirmation cannot be understood in its entirety without intensely contemplating it through the practice of magick.

As the student progresses in their magickal path, their under-standing of the core meaning of magick and of how it works also improves, gaining new and previously unthought depth.

By changing the inside, the outside changes as well. It is a miracle that we want each student of magick to discover experientially for themselves.

SECTION 2
The Foundation

6

Magickal Preparation

When we perform magick, we have one of these two purposes:

A- *To improve the self's personality or cause some change in mundane life unrelated to mystical growth.*

E.g., fulfill a mundane desire, attract riches, or achieve a more materialistic goal.

B- *To transcend the self or cause some change in a context of mystical or spiritual growth.*

E.g., fulfill a spiritually elevating desire, develop or acquire a mystical virtue, dissolve a flaw that blocks magickal progress, connect with the Higher Self, access collective states of mind, obtain transpersonal consciousness, perform deep subconscious transformation, purify or heal the psyche, ascend individuality into universality, tap into universal knowledge, experience bliss, raptures, infinity, or anything whose purpose is to achieve a mystical or spiritual goal.

Most magickal books concern "A" and totally disregard "B". This is a mistake. Our material existence mustn't be ignored, but neither should our immortal and divine identity.

Magick Rituals

Rituals are at the heart of magick. It is by performing rituals that we accomplish many of our magickal goals. But what is a magick ritual?

In this volume, a ritual is a set of magickal procedures or acts that someone performs in order to cause a change. This change can be physical, emotional, energetic, mental, or spiritual. In the physical realm, some of our desired changes are seemingly outside of our reach, but we can directly affect and modify the subtler planes, which then trigger a shift in the grosser planes, manifesting the wanted outcome.

At its core, magick is to be practiced, not theorized about or intellectually understood. It shouldn't be learned in abstract terms but experienced and lived. More than giving automatic results, it is an ongoing experimentation and investigation of ourselves and the cosmos.

Preconditions

Before addressing the main magickal practices and rituals, there needs to be a solid base in certain abilities. These are:

- Observational Concentration
- Relaxation
- Awareness of the Vital Force
- Self-contemplation
- Awakening the Inner Vision

Developing a reasonable degree of proficiency in these areas through meditative and mystical practice dramatically improves your chances of success in magick.

If you have read and/or practiced the methods laid out in *The Art of Mysticism* or *The Art of Occultism*, then you are already well-prepared. Both of these books give sound foundations (and more), which are often underestimated but are critical in successfully practicing magick. Nonetheless, it's important to do the prefatory phase to get the body and mind in the right condition, mindset, and state for actual magick.

All of these five abilities are interconnected, so despite approaching them individually, improving one will enhance all the others and so on.

1) Observational Concentration

Having mastery over thoughts is necessary for a successful magickal practice.

Procedure:

Sit or lie down and take a few deep breaths. Close your eyes, relax the body, and notice what's happening in your mind.

Initially, you will recognize that thoughts seem to flood your mind from all angles. These thoughts are probably composed of worries, everyday affairs, plans for the future, etc. Don't resist those thoughts, merely observe them, and let them be. According to the mental situation you happen to be in at the moment, this exercise will be more or less easy for you.

After a while, you will notice that you have lost track of what you were doing (observing the mind). If that happens, once you become conscious that you are off-course, come back to an observational position. Thoughts will not be merciful; they shall rush into you with uncontrollable speed and strength.

Gradually, you shall notice an improvement in this practice: the mind will become less turbulent, thoughts become fewer and fewer, and at last, the mind becomes clear and nearly thought-free.

Once you are able to observe your thoughts for five straight minutes without losing track of what you are doing (maintaining watchfulness), your observational concentration has acquired an initial level of stabilization that will prove to be useful in magickal practice. More is better, of course.

This practice must be completed twice per day. You can also try to do it 2/3 times in a row, but remember that you must complete five minutes of thought-observation without wandering off. You can also increase the practice's amount of time, should it not suffice. Beware of falling asleep while doing this exercise.

Students should, on no account, proceed further into the main magickal practices until this 5-minute observational concentration preparation has been achieved. Thought control and thought-detachment are an essential component of magic development, and must never be skipped.

Students must be able to meditate and perform rituals without having their minds filled with worries or thoughts about their day jobs, personal problems, family dramas, and so on. When a student is performing magick, all of their mental content must be related to magick and spiritual evolution, otherwise, what they will accomplish is a deeper degree of mind-wandering and daydreaming.

As a supplementary practice, students can also perform exclusive attention techniques, such as choosing a thought, mental image, or an object, and focusing on it. If required, thoughts that keep rising must be suppressed. This shouldn't be done by giving them attention and then trying to eliminate them, but by paying attention, over and over again, to the chosen object or single thought. At first, the student will probably succeed only for a few seconds, but with time and given sufficient practice, five minutes of single-focus attention will be achieved.

Mastering this precondition (observational concentration) is absolutely indispensable. All magickal practices depend on it. It is not an easy task by any means, and most students give up here, but it's a requirement for successful magick practice. The more thought-free and single-focused your attention is, the better chances of having profound magickal results.

2) Relaxation

Full body relaxation is also imperative.

Procedure:

1. Sit down with a good posture, or lie down, take a deep breath, and relax.

2. While inhaling, tense your feet, and then while exhaling, relax them. Next, take another breath in and tense your calves and then relax them while breathing out. Keep doing this method of inhaling and tensing, exhaling and releasing/relaxing, and apply it to the thighs, hips, glutes, stomach, chest, upper back, hands, arms, neck, jaw, face, and head. Pay particular attention to the relaxing motion and feeling when you let your muscles completely relax after tensing them.

Continue doing this for 2-3 rounds to get your muscles fully relaxed. If possible, wear loose and comfortable clothing. Tight clothes may restrict blood circulation and the flow of energy.

The ability to relax is a skill just like any other, and it can be learned progressively. In the beginning, it will take a lot of time to deeply relax, and it can lead to sleep, boredom, dreaming, etc., diminishing your enthusiasm. But if you approach it with the correct mindset, you will be able to achieve a good degree of deep physical relaxation in a few weeks.

Profound physical relaxation opens the gates of the mystical trance state. In this state, the student's consciousness operates at a much higher level, and because of this, their magickal practices will be much more powerful and efficient.

3) Self-Contemplation

All traditions stress the importance of knowing who we are. Without self-knowledge, there can hardly be any development in higher levels.

The student must use the two previous acquired abilities, observational concentration, and deep relaxation, to look back at himself.

Procedure:

Sit in a quiet place and meditate by reflecting on your personality. Which traits do usually hold you back? What kind of fears do you have? Why aren't you achieving what you truly desire? Notice all sorts of ugly habits and traits without embellishing any of them. Picture yourself, in your mind, into various negative past situations and recall how you acted and what mistakes, shadow aspects, or flaws emerged during those times.

Becoming aware of your failures, weaknesses, and shortcomings will make you more self-aware, thereby adequately preparing you to face the unexpected nature of magick. Whenever an unprepared neophyte is practicing magick, they may be easily startled, fear may quickly arise, and the whole practice or ritual will collapse.

The deeper you can probe into your psyche and illuminate it with understanding, the better you'll perform your magickal practices.

Self-contemplation is one of the most pivotal yet neglected areas of magickal preparation. Through this self-reflection exercise, you can learn a great deal about yourself, delving deep into your subconscious mind. What began as a simple look into your personality and traits turns into an inquiry into the psychological roots of your identity. This will require alertness, patience, and a powerful will, but if neglected, magickal results will be poor.

This shadow-observance endeavor functions as a preparatory cleaning device, helping the student acquire an initial psychological equilibrium. Therefore, you ought to devote some minutes to self-contemplation in the morning and at night.

There's no amount of time scheduled for this exercise, but it should be done regularly. Further magickal advancement depends on it.

4) Awareness of the Vital Force

Breathing is a semiconscious process that occurs in all human beings. Through unconscious breathing, the body gets the bare minimum vitality, which is not sufficient for students who want to raise substantial amounts of energy for magickal practice and rituals. Therefore, as a means of boosting energy and vitality, the student must learn how to consciously breathe and become aware of the vital force that runs through the energy body. Being aware of this force will enable the student to use it during magickal rituals.

Procedure:

1- Sit down in a comfortable position, close your eyes, and

relax your body by inhaling through the nose and exhaling through the mouth.

2- Do this for around five minutes.

3- Once you are relaxed enough, visualize radiant white energy rising from the bottom of the spinal cord, going upwards around the back until the top of the head while inhaling, and then, going down through the front of the body while exhaling, until it reaches the coccyx.

This energy will begin to surround your whole body until you get into a deep and relaxed energetic state. Your body may also begin to feel very light.

Do this for 10 to 20 minutes.

Given sufficient practice, you will begin to sense the vital force within your body and around in your aura. You may feel tingling all over the body, goosebumps, shivering energy through the spinal cord, or any type of energetic effect.

5) *Awakening the Inner Eye*

Visualization and vivid imagination are indispensable tools in Magickal practice and rituals. Students of magick must strive to improve their inner vision by any means necessary, to the best of their ability.

Procedure:

1. Sit in your standard meditation posture and close the eyes;

2. Take five deep breaths to soothe body and mind;

3. Touch the space between the eyebrows with your index finger. Apply some pressure. Once that is done, drop the hand to its normal position.

4. Center your attention on the space between the eyebrows.

5. Imagine that you are breathing through the space between the eyebrows (even though you are breathing through the nose). Feel energy moving in and out as you inhale and exhale. Do it for 3 to 5 minutes.

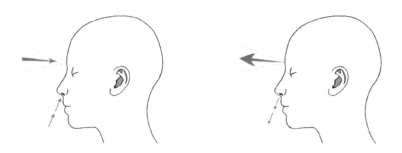

6. Afterwards, when inhaling, visualize golden energy coming from the source of the universe, accumulating between the eyebrows. When exhaling, see the third eye shining in bright golden light, as if it were the sun. You should feel a little pressure there, in the third eye. Keep doing this for 10 to 20 minutes.

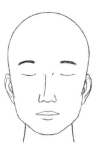

Over time, as you continue employing this technique, you will begin to feel pressure or tingling in this area. It may take days, weeks, or months. You are dealing with subtle perceptions, consequently, sensations may initially be faint. The flow of energy and the intensity of the pressure may also vary from day to day, so if the energy and intensity don't seem powerful enough in one day, it does not imply that something is going awry. All students should maintain their motivation and commitment regardless of the daily outcome.

Given sufficient practice, you will begin to see visual symbols, geometric patterns, and even lifelike images in your mind's eye. In due course, you will be able to connect your inner and outer vision, overlapping astral images into gross physical perception. This is a very valuable skill in magick rituals.

Conclusion to the Preconditions

All of these preparatory exercises should be done for three to six months, on average, before proceeding into the practice of magick rituals. If you've already practiced what's taught in *The Art of Mysticism* or *The Art of Occultism*, then your preparatory period will be shorter. Nonetheless, no student should go further into magick without having completed these exercises.

All of these skills are thoroughly important, and they must be learned correctly, otherwise the student will sooner or later face a stumbling block that will force him to come back to these fundamentals. Without success in these exercises, actual deep magick will seldom be successful.

7

Dissecting the Core of Magick

Most of the time, practical magick is used as the path for enhancing selfishness and growing self-importance and false knowledge. There are plenty of magickal books with descriptions on how to do such-and-such magick to achieve such-and-such results.

Instead of addressing lower forms of magick in this book, we have decided to teach the highest and the most conducive magickal practices that will contribute to real mystical and spiritual transformation and transcendence. All great magicians use magick as the medium for spiritual emancipation or to improve their physical, emotional, mental, and energetic bodies to become vessels of divinity.

Nonetheless, understanding the methodology and components of a well-structured magick ritual is fundamental for both its creation and practice. Even though creating your own may seem daunting or impossible at first, once you understand its core, creating rituals gets quite straightforward, and you can then use them for any purpose you desire. The degree of integrity or concerning their goal will be in your hands.

Designing Magick Rituals

Magick rituals are the crux of magick. They induce a deep level of consciousness that enables students to intensely focus their whole will and intention into a purpose, thereby directing their subconscious and conscious mind and energy into initiating the manifestation of that intention. When a practitioner of magickal arts is performing a ritual, it's just as if they were speaking with the cosmos, asking for the manifestation of an intention.

To comprehend the core of a magickal ritual, students must delve into it and understand how it's made. Though there are countless variables, there are three main ingredients in every one of them:

1. The practitioner must be in an altered state of consciousness, typically higher than the regular day-to-day consciousness.

2. The practitioner must have a clear-cut intention and goal on what they want to achieve with the magickal ritual.

3. The practitioner must know how to use energy and symbolic representational forces to direct their intention into the manifestation of the chosen goal.

If a student can put all of these principles into action, then they can do any type of magick ritual. They can also use external objects, but that's generally nonessential if the use of inner tools is powerful enough.

Each mystical tradition and discipline have their methods of:

1. Getting into an alternate state of consciousness or trance;

2. Directing the intention and will;

3. Using energy, forces, and symbolism to put in motion the manifestation of the goal.

By learning the methodology on how to create your own rituals, you can create one according to your predispositions and preferences. Ultimately, the only difference is in the presentation of the "final package", in its style and design, rather than on its core, which is what fundamentally matters.

Instead of rehashing the traditional style of rituals that use external objects and magickal tools (which are often difficult for neophytes to consecrate correctly), the student will use other types of objects and tools. External tools can be useful as symbolic representations of our will or of the ceremonial action that sets in motion our intention, but they draw their power from our will, emotion, intention, vital force, and mind. Why then use intermediaries when we have direct access to the source?

This is not the conventional way of performing magickal rituals, but we have found it to be a superior way, if the student acquires the required depth and ability.

Entering Into the Ritual:

Before plunging into the methods of achieving a higher state of consciousness for magick ritual performance, we have to address the opening of rituals. This is to be done before the ritual starts, and before achieving a higher state of consciousness. If the practitioner is still a neophyte, this should be done before practicing the techniques to alter the state of consciousness, to teach the mind that this is a trigger to get into a higher state of consciousness.

You can design your own way of opening the ritual. To do so, choose something that brings a mystical and pleasurable feeling, a rush of enthusiasm, respect, divinity, and gratitude. In the beginning, you can simply perform a hand gesture, do a particular movement, use a meditation bell, or repeat a mantra or sacred word three times.

With sufficient practice, just by the act of opening the ritual, the student will instantly enter into a higher state of consciousness because they have conditioned the mind to go into that state after the opening of the ritual.

Exiting the Ritual:

Just like there's an act to enter into the magick ritual, there's one to exit. After the ritual has been performed, the practitioner shouldn't merely walk away. There must be a trigger that will help their consciousness return to its standard daily level, so that the practitioner can continue living daily life and perform mundane tasks as well as fulfilling worldly responsibilities, instead of being "lost" drifting in mystical realms and states. Without closing the ritual, the practitioner's energy may also become highly imbalanced.

Each ritual requires a finishing "action" that brings consciousness back to its ordinary level of functioning, grounding the student back into the physical world. If possible, it should always be the inverse of the opening technique, and just like the opening, it should always be the same method, so that it is easier to remember and execute. However, if it's not possible to reverse the opening method, (e.g., if it is chanting *Aum* three times), then when the student opens the session, they can accompany it with some physical or mental movement that has a reverse action, like slowing opening the hands when chanting *Aum*, and then when exiting, chanting *Aum* while closing the hands.

Sometimes, while performing the ritual, the practitioner will be in such a profound and altered state that it won't be easy to return to an ordinary state. Having such a trigger makes sure one will always come back after finishing the ritual. Once the practitioner comes back, they must breathe normally and feel the physical body. When they feel grounded, they can resume regular life.

Phase One: Magickal Trance

Whenever a student of magick wants to achieve something, the most critical aspect is to change their inner state so that their actions, thoughts, emotions, energy, and internal state begin to vibrate in the frequency that will better manifest the desired outcome. Magickal rituals begin by inducing a higher state of consciousness, in which a student can correctly perform magick. Entering into a higher state of consciousness is essential to the correct practice of magick.

The higher states of consciousness are not only for saints and mystics, but they're available to every practitioner. When they are achieved, the practitioner's perception of reality dramatically shifts, and one may sense or perceive things that until then were unseen and unthought of. Magick flows immensely better in a higher state.

When students are absorbed in and entertained by their scattered thoughts and everyday affairs, magick will not be effective or powerful. They need to clear their minds of these distractions to perform magick to the best of their ability (the preparatory practices are fundamental for this).

Nonetheless, even though a practitioner is still aware of the world around himself when performing magick, it fades into the background, opening the expanse of the inner world and higher realms, getting him closer to interacting with subtle energies, entities, and forces.

This state is one where the student's conscious mind is immersed in the subconscious, but it is not like daydreaming or hallucinating. It is much more awake, controlled, lucid, and profound. It can be called "Magickal Trance". Different traditions employ different methods of achieving such a state:

- Repeating mental or vocal syllabus or words (magickal mantras, mystic prayer, magickal sounds, and divine chants);

- Repeated breathing patterns (shamanic breathing, yogic breathing, tibetan breathing, and mystical breathing);

- Repeated movements (tribal rituals, and mystic dance);

- Extreme continuous focus on inner or outer visual imagery;

- Repeated imagined sensations (mentally falling or going downstairs).

Considering this, students can create their own method of entering into a higher level of consciousness, as long as it's built on a repetitive motion (physical, energetical, or mental). If you've done the practices of *The Art of Mysticism* or *The Art of Occultism*, you can also use them here, as they put you into a higher state of consciousness. However, you don't generally need to reach a trance so deep that your body is asleep and your mind awake, as it's required for some of the practices in these books.

In the next part, you will find different methodologies that you can execute or use as a base to create your own. All of them require good concentration and relaxation skills. Don't let your mind drift off, or instead of inducing a trance state, you will succumb to slumber.

All of the trance inducing methods should start by sitting in the standard meditation posture, closing the eyes, and taking a couple of deep breaths.

If any of these following practices are done correctly, you will be in a higher state of consciousness. Once you finish any of them, your mind is calmer, your consciousness has bridged into the subconscious, your mental abilities are sharpened, and you are in a better state to perform magick.

a) Magickal Mantra

Many people swear by the use of some specific mantra, but we suggest that each student chooses one that fits their mental inclination.

Procedure (Vocal):

1. Repeat the selected mantra mentally, over and over again for about 20 to 30 minutes. Every time you lose the mantra, merely come back to it. The speed or rhythm that you employ does not matter.

2. In the course of time, you will notice that you are automatically and effortlessly chanting the mantra. It repeats itself. You should then merely observe the mantra go on and on by itself.

After the meditation is over, stay in your current posture, resting for 5 minutes. Don't do anything in particular, just rest.

Procedure (Mental):

1. Repeat the selected mantra mentally, over and over again for about 20 to 30 minutes. Every time you lose the

mantra, merely come back to it. The speed or rhythm that you employ does not matter.

2. In the course of time, the mind itself will take the mantra, and it goes on repeating these mental syllables automatically. You should then merely observe the mantra go on and on by itself.

After the practice is over, stay in your current posture, resting for 5 minutes. Don't do anything in particular, just rest.

b) Shamanic Breathing

In this method, you shouldn't sit down, but instead, lay down on your back.

Procedure:

1. Take a few deep breaths through the nose and relax your body.

2. Do a two-second inhalation followed by a two-second exhalation without any gaps between both. As soon as you finish inhaling, you must exhale, and vice versa. Use your abdomen to make your stomach expand and contract with each inhalation and exhalation.

3. Keep breathing quickly with two-second inhalations and exhalations but don't create any tension. Find your own rhythm.

After 10 to 20 minutes, your body may be tingling, and you may experience a feeling of rapture. Your consciousness has temporarily risen to a higher level.

c) *Mystic Breath*

Any type of restrained breathing, such as "Pranayama" techniques, alter your state of consciousness. They relax the body and mind by slow and controlled breathing. With a calm breath, the mind will automatically be quiet as well. The Mystic Breath is a form of breath-restraint that raises the student's level of consciousness.

It has proven to be a great help to all those who resort to it, calming their mind, reducing the amount of mental chaos, lowering the heart rate and the metabolism by lengthening the breath, helping the body reach a deep state of relaxation with extreme ease, thus relieving accumulated tensions and so on and so forth.

The Mystic Breath can also aid the student to perceive the flow of the vital force coursing through the body (as an alternative practice to the preliminary method of Awareness of the Vital Force). The soothing sound, pressure and vibrations make it the perfect practice to alter consciousness into a deeper state.

This type of breathing produces a very characteristic oceanic sound, and for that reason, many different traditions call it the breath of the ocean.

To produce this sound and vibration, it is sufficient to constrict the back of the throat lightly while inhaling or exhaling. However, we will present more detailed instructions that will allow the student to learn how to do it.

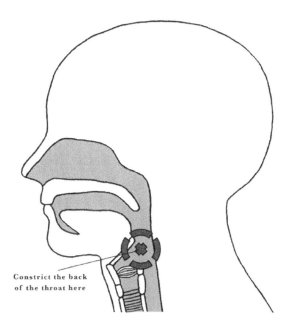

Constrict the back
of the throat here

Technique:

1. Open your mouth and expel the air as if you were fog-ging up a mirror.

2. Repeat the same type of exhalation by placing the hand extended in front of the mouth. Pay particular attention to the warm air touching your hand.

3. Repeat the exhalation but with the mouth closed. Exhale through the nostrils.

4. Next, inhale while maintaining the contraction of the epiglottis. It will make a similar sound to the sound of the exhalation.

5. Fully breathe while maintaining the back of the throat contracted at all times.

Procedure:

1. Do the Mystic Breath for 20 to 30 minutes. Enjoy the pleasurable sensations that the Mystic Breath produces in your body.

2. After finishing, remain in your current posture and enjoy the feelings and sensations in your body. See how much calmer, peaceful, and joyful you are. Your state of consciousness is now much higher.

d) Magickal Sound

Any variety of sacred chanting or singing, tribal drumming, and some types of repetitive rhythms made by instruments can get the student into a meditative state of consciousness, as the rhythmic flow and beat of the music elevates it.

e) Shamanic Movements

Some movements, when repeated accurately, can induce an altered state of consciousness (e.g., dance, yogic asanas, or even some forms of exercise).

An effective mystical technique is the shamanic method of the Head's Circular Dance:

Procedure:

1. With the eyes closed, look at the top of your head and focus there.

2. Rest the chin on your chest.

3. Perform the head movement, as explained in the following image. There should be no bouncing. Additionally, perform a long vocalization during each movement, as shown in the image.

This means that as you move your head, you chant the following mantras for 2 seconds:

- front "Iiiii" (lengthening the "I" as in **I**ndia)
- left, "Ooooo" (lengthening the "O" as in **O**rlando);
- back, "Aaaaa" (lengthening the "A" as in **A**ffair);
- right, "Eeeee" (lengthening the "E" as in **E**lephant);
- front, back to the starting position, "Iiiii".

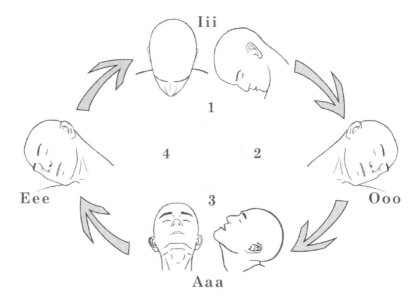

1) The head begins by resting the chin on the chest.

2) The head moves to the left shoulder (the left ear moves towards the left shoulder).

3) The head tilts back.

4) The head moves to the right shoulder (the right ear moves towards the right shoulder).

After step 4, the head moves from the right shoulder towards the initial position.

One round takes about 10 seconds. Perform this for 10 to 20 minutes. Be careful with your neck. Do the movements very delicately without hurrying.

f) Left-Path Tantric Movements

Some traditions use intercourse and inner orgasms as the means to reach a deeper state of consciousness. This is out of the scope of this volume, but we considered it important to mention.

g) Visual Focus

Choose an object that embodies something mystical or spiritual to you. It can also be a symbol rather than actual objects, but they must be drawn on a paper and framed.

Procedure:

1. Place the object in the correct position and sit comfortably in a straight-backed chair, sofa, mat, or on a meditation cushion. If it's not an object that you are capable of positioning, such as a statue, merely posture yourself correctly in a favorable position for steady gazing. The correct posture includes having the spine erect.

2. Relax the body.

3. Focus on the chosen object for 10 minutes with the eyes opened. Keep the mind focused on that point as if only that object existed in the whole universe.

As you keep on practicing, self-pace and gradually increase the minutes until you can do it for around 20 to 30 minutes without much disturbing thoughts or distractions. Remember to relax the eyes to prevent them from flickering. Do not try not to blink. You may naturally blink to hydrate the eyes, but there may come a time that many minutes go by without blinking.

Instead of using a physical object, you can also visualize the object or symbol in your mind's eye and perform the same practice, but with the eyes closed. You can alternate between both, as they will have the same intended effect of elevating your consciousness.

h) Imagined Sensations

In both of these methods, the student uses their imagination and kinesthetic sensations to fall into a deeper state of consciousness.

Falling Method

In this method, you must lay down on your back.

Take a few deep breaths and imagine the sensation of falling. Feel yourself falling, deeper, and deeper. Notice how your body seems to melt, relaxing more and more with each exhalation and falling sensation. Keep falling, going deeper and deeper every time, until you enter into a magickal trance.

Going Downstairs Method

Imagine standing at the top of a lengthy staircase. Begin walking down at a slow pace, step by step, one at a time. Feel the downward motion as you keep descending one step at a time. Go deeper into yourself. Feel your body becoming heavier and heavier. Repeat this process until you enter into a magickal trance.

These are some of the methods to achieve a higher state of consciousness that improve your ability to perform deep magick. Typically, deep trance or higher states of consciousness are achieved only through sitting meditation. However, in magick, we are not aiming to induce states where the body falls asleep or is paralyzed, but only to get into a higher state of consciousness where the body retails full functions in order to perform magick. Once the student achieves such a state, they should take a few moments to rest in it, feeling aware, focused, relaxed, and ready to engage in magick.

There are also other, more radical or violent methods of achieving an alternate state of consciousness, such as extreme fasting, total isolation, psychedelics, pain (e.g., scourging), etc., but we will not address them in this volume as they are not the most appropriate for this type of deep magickal work.

Ultimately, given sufficient practice, you may be able to alter your consciousness at will. That's one of the real virtues of a magician.

Phase Two: Will, Intention, and Goal

The next step in designing a magickal ritual is answering the simple questions: What is the goal? What do you want to accomplish with this ritual?

Before setting the wheels of manifestation in motion, you must know what you desire. Your intentions must be so limpid that your will to achieve it pierces through all the blockages that you may encounter. Furthermore, the goal must be clear, and it must be instilled into the subconscious.

If your intentions are unclear, then the outcome will be fragile and impotent. Through your will and intention, you set in motion the process by which the magick act will bring about the manifestation of the goal. You are shaping and creating that reality for yourself, or in other words, your state of being begins to vibrate in a frequency harmonized with the goal, bringing it into your reality.

If you want to use magick to fulfill personal desires, then you must be careful with what you desire. If you are overly specific, you can block possible pathways for the manifestation of a greater result, yet if you aren't specific enough, your desire may be unclear. It's a delicate process. You must also affirm the intention as if the goal has already been achieved, such as "I am..." or "I have..." instead of "I want...".

Furthermore, even though you can begin by using affirmations and writing down your goal, specific desires are mostly expressed through feeling and emotion. It's the inner feeling and emotion that are the most effective, instead of just words. Words work primarily on a conscious level, while feeling and emotion bring the subconscious into action, making the magick ritual much more powerful.

Many people who read magickal books seek magick for things such as financial independence or to manifest material abundance. It must be underlined that this work is not about such goals. We understand the importance of mundane desires and objectives, but students of Deep Magick aim to reach unseen magickal depths that go much further into the divine.

Magick is captivating because it brings us towards divinity, surpassing all our mundane expectations and goals. Goals for genuine magickal rituals must not be taken lightly.

Though any student can use magick to improve the self in the most selfish or mundane manners, this is not really what genuine magick is about. There are countless magickal books about these subjects, but are they more than cheap gimmicks that feed off people's insecurities and lack of emotional fulfillment? They don't aim at solving the root cause of the problem, but at masking symptoms. If a student wants to find a love partner, they should do magick that helps them to become the best version of themselves; if they want to earn money, instead of doing magick to win the lottery, they should do magick that develops their abilities to work harder and better at their job or business, such as improving thought-clarity, proactiveness, vitality, concentration, creativity, problem-solving capabilities, etc. Ultimately, the trick is not to use magick for avarice or as a masking agent, but as a tool for self-improvement and self-transcendence.

Fierce Intention

More vital than effort, visualization, or concentration, is knowing what you truly want. If you are perfectly conscious of what you want with all parts of your multidimensional being, then magick is that final push that will get your desired outcome manifested.

It's worth taking time to understand and discover what you honestly want. This may seem simple at first glance, but sometimes, your real intention lies behind a false desire. You may think that you desire a million dollars, but what you really want is freedom or security, the freedom and security that having that money provides (e.g., not having to go to work for someone else doing something that you don't enjoy, and being able to improve your and your family's health and wellbeing). You may think that you desire to take some spectacular vacations in the Maldives, but what you really want is peace of mind, a stress-free environment, and a relaxed life. Many students waste energy and time pursuing desires through magick that they don't truly want.

Magick is much less likely to work, and may actually make you feel low, if your intention and will are not truly aligned with your authentic desires and objectives. This can be an illuminative experience because, in such instance, magick will help you find out your true will and intention, giving you an outcome that compels you to look in the mirror.

When magick is performed to accomplish a legitimate desire or intention, the results can be swift and remarkable, but magick may also bring some changes that you weren't expecting. There's also the possibility that magick offers you something deeper than what you originally wanted or greater than your initial goal. You may think that the magick didn't work, but you're actually being bestowed with something much better than what you originally wanted. Don't ignore or reject that. It may be frightening, but it may just be the next big step in your mystical path.

Ego Will and Divine Will

The universe has a way of balancing things out. Some may call this *karma*, while others, *destiny*. Using the preceding example, if someone wants to become financially wealthy and undertakes magickal rituals to achieve that goal, a successful outcome may also bring other "elements" along with money, such as suffering or misery. A practitioner can never know how those outcomes may affect their life. Typically, when executing personal-will rituals, the practitioner surely believe that they are mostly for the better, but sometimes, they may bring bittersweet results. To give an example, following the previous case, becoming financially wealthy and independent may also bring over-whelming new responsibilities that will prevent the student from committing to himself to the art of magick, impeding further spiritual progress.

It's important to seriously think about the profound ramifications of the magick that you're going to perform.

That's why we always suggest that students disregard mate-rialistic and egoic desires. Nonetheless, as long as they don't push the student away from divinity into egocentricity, by increasing attachment to material wealth, a few rituals to improve some mundane aspects of life do no harm.

Magick rituals should be used mostly to the pursuit of God, the Source of everything, and to perfect our multidimensional being to embody divinity.

Real magicians use magick to fulfill their will according to their Higher Self or Divine Will instead of for selfish pursuits. Magick, when performed from your deepest will, is just much more powerful, effective, and in a much higher vibration than magick for personal or egoic gains. Again, magick for personal gain is not bad (unless used to harm or disrupt others, which may backfire), but it just isn't as mighty, efficient, and life-changing as using magick for the fulfillment of the Divine Will.

However, sometimes, the exploration of will that doesn't have divine grounds can be a good way of finding out the highest will. Students may now understand the importance of the practice of self-introspection, instructed in the Preconditions. Without self-introspection, no student can really know their true will and desires. It may be useful to practice it again, at this time.

Ultimately, if you can get into a higher state of consciousness and affirm your will with all of your senses, emotion, and being, emanating a clear intention and goal, magick rituals become an extraordinary tool in your mystical repertoire. You just need to know what you truly want.

Phase Three: Energy, Force, and Manifestation

The final component of creating our own rituals is being able to control and use energy, and direct it towards the manifestation of our goal.

By achieving a higher state of consciousness, we can access and tap into subtle forms of energy that facilitate the accomplishment of our intention. It's a process of connecting and gathering the correct energy, and then launching it into Creation to manifest the chosen intention.

To succeed in doing this, we need the source of the energy, and the intermediary between our conscious will and the universal mind through which the energy will be channeled.

Just as in the techniques to achieve altered states of consciousness, to be able to direct and manipulate energy, different traditions and disciplines use a combination of various methods and sources. Some of the methods may seem similar, like employing a mantra, using visualizations, kinesthetic awareness, etc., but the purpose for which they are employed is entirely different.

Proficiency in the preliminary practice of becoming aware of the vital force is essential for this phase. The vital force has been called numerous names by different traditions, such as *ki*, *chi*, *prana*, vital force, *pneuma*, *ruach*, and so on.

Despite the labels, there are countless forms of energy; some have been mapped out by modern science, such as those on the electromagnetic spectrum, while others are strikingly subtle and yet to be fully understood or comprehended except for those who set sail into spiritual, mystical, and occult paths.

Because of the interaction of the immaterial consciousness with the physical body, subtle energy is created that flows through the body at different dimensional levels. Students with some degree of sensitivity can sense it. It flows through the nervous system, and at a subtler level, at what many call the energy body and spiritual vortexes.

Then, there's also universal energy, which is not within the body but propagates throughout the universe like the background cosmic radiation (at a grosser level). These are the two main energies that students of magick work with in magick rituals. This means that the source of energy for magickal rituals will either be the practitioner's own vital force or universal energy.

To effectively gather and direct energy towards the goal, the student also needs to learn about the "receiver" of that energy: Magick Seals. These seals receive energy and work as powerful transmitters and amplifiers of energy. They help transmute energy from our individual, personal fields, into the universal, impersonal field, or vice versa.

Magickal Seals

Magickal symbols are indispensable in rituals because they allow students to harness and direct subtle forces within Creation. They are the interface that allows us to work with the subtle energy and elements of Creation. They function as the intermediary between the student's conscious will and the universal mind through which the energy will be channeled.

Our subconscious mind is the part of our being that is connected to the subtler dimensions of Creation (i.e., the subtler aspects of the universal mind). It doesn't understand words but images. To communicate more efficiently with those subtler dimensions, practitioners use magickal symbols.

Each symbol represents a particular type of energy, and the more your mind sees it and interacts with it, the more it is strengthened, increasing your connection and the possibility of manifesting your will.

Mystical traditions have different systems of symbology (e.g., Jewish Mysticism has Kabbalah, with Sephirot, Angels, etc.; Hinduism has Yoga, with Chakras, Deities, etc.), and all have their merit and power. They are all forms of mystical and magickal work, but ultimately, none is better than the other. It's the student's predisposition that will lead them to some particular type of symbols and systems.

We do not subscribe to any tradition in particular, as they all come with their unique dogmas and limitations. Though many may view this as sacrilege, it is entirely acceptable to combine different symbologies and systems, as long as they work.

For example, you can use yoga breathing techniques to enter into an alternate state of consciousness (Yogic system), call the names of Angels in your magickal rituals to help manifest your goal (anthropomorphized Mystical Judaic symbolic system), and use tantric techniques for the accumulation and direction of energy. If it works, nobody is going to be burned for heresy.

Understanding Magickal Symbology

A picture is worth a thousand words.

When we see any form of advertising, more than words, we see a logo, an image, or a symbol. As we see that symbol over and over again, we begin to associate it with that brand and with whatever it is that they do. As its connection and energy begin to build up, it is stored in our subconscious mind. Given it is assimilated into sufficient people, it goes into the collective unconscious of humanity, and it gains a life of its own. This implies that it doesn't matter what someone thinks or feels that the symbol conveys because its collective energy and meaning overpowers everyone's individual power in magickal practice.

The following symbols are examples of powerful mystical and magickal symbols that convey much more than words could do:

For instance, practitioners can't use the *Om* symbol to perform negative magick. They may think it will work, but in the long run, it won't. Students may find written in other magick books that divine energy and symbols may successfully be used for malevolent purposes, but although it may initially look like they will work in the short-term, they wind up not working, creating karmic repercussions and backlashing against the practitioner (directly or indirectly) in the long haul.

All symbols can be categorized into "Divine"/"Benevolent", "Neutral"/"Latent", or "Evil-minded"/"Malevolent". If the Om symbol is unquestionably divine and benevolent, something like the *Tarot*, which is a vast treasure of magickal symbolism, is neutral and latent. That is to say, it is capable of being used for both divine or bad-natured purposes.

Some symbols convey dreadfully negative energy, such as the Nazi symbol, which is a distortion of the sacred *swastika* of Hinduism. Because it's so ingrained into the human collective unconscious, practitioners can't perform magick with the Nazi's symbol for positive or divine purposes. It won't work. Its collective energy and meaning will overpower practitioners' individual energy and significance.

To overcome the collective mind and change the energy and meaning of a symbol, students would need an extreme amount of magickal power, and it would still take a great deal of time (i.e., lifetimes). A symbol with hundreds or thousands of years, or one that has left a deep scar in humanity's soul, can't be changed overnight.

Entities, spirits, beings, deities, angels, etc., can also work as the intermediary between one's conscious will and the universal mind through which the energy will be channeled. Instead of using Magick Seals, we request the help of nonphysical entities to achieve our goal.

Choosing the Right Magickal Seal

The chosen symbol must be a representation of the student's desired outcome. Each magickal seal is capable of conveying much more information, feeling, and energy than words.

Practitioners can pick any already-existing symbol if it aligns with their intentions and desired outcome, otherwise they will have to create their own to use it in magickal practices.

Creating your own is easy. First, you need to understand what your seal will convey. What is it that you want to do? What is your goal? What's the ultimate purpose of this symbol? Sit down and contemplate on what you want to achieve with this magickal symbol.

Once you are clear about these answers, grab a paper and design a symbol that represents the result of what you want to achieve. Here's how each student should do it:

1- You're doing magick to elicit a change. What change is this? Feel your desire, goal, purpose, or intention.

2- Then, design a symbol that represents the achievement of that desire, goal, purpose, or intention, and frame it.

3- Sit on your standard meditation position, and focus on that symbol with the intention that you want to imbue it with.

Focus on the goal being achieved within your body and mind; breathe the goal being achieved; imagine the goal being achieved; feel the goal being achieved; see it being totally and utterly accomplished and successful. Allow yourself to feel the pleasure of having achieved the goal. Notice your emotional reaction and current state of mind. Concentrate all of that energy into the symbol.

4- Meditate on that symbol for about 10 days, 30 minutes per day, permeating it with the intended energy. Use emotion. The seal gathers energy every time you do it, getting more and more infused with your intention.

After the 10 days, it can be used in magickal rituals.

Connecting the Dots

Students should do their magick ritual in a specific place used exclusively for rituals, meditation, or mystical and spiritual practice (such as a Laboratorium as taught in *The Art of Occultism*). They can adorn it with candles, incense, drawings of the magick seal, etc.

Things that have to be done beforehand, as they've been explained in the past chapters:

- Having checked all preconditions through the preliminary practices;

- Having your whole-being intention/goal decided and rooted in the subconscious;

- Having your Magick Seal charged and ready;

- Being capable of entering into a higher state of consciousness without losing body-awareness or entering into a trance so deep that you can't move.

Basic Procedure:

1. Enter into a higher state of consciousness using your pre-ferred method.

2. Initiate the ritual with the chosen method of entering. You can be sitting or standing.

3. With your eyes closed, visualize your Magick Seal using your inner eye to the best of your ability.

If it's magick to *improve the self's personality or cause some change in mundane life unrelated to mystical growth*, you must connect your own energy with the Magick Seal's energy by focusing on it, and then absorb the Seal into your own being (if it's to change the self's personality in some way) or expand it into the universe to manifest the required external change (e.g., to manifest an external or materialistic goal).

If it's magick to *transcend the self or cause some change in a context of mystical or spiritual growth*, you will use universal energy by absorbing it from the chosen Magick Seal, and then assimilate it into yourself with the intention of achieving the proposed goal of inner change and transcendence. Chapter 8 on Deep Magick has various examples of this type of magick rituals.

4. Once it is done, exit the ritual with the chosen method of closing.

Don't spend the rest of the day thinking or doubting the efficacy of the magick ritual. Usually, the bigger the goal, the less quickly it will manifest. Each situation or student's karma is different, so depending on the goal and other variables, the effect may be quite sudden or take months. Nonetheless, you must be confident in your magick and know that if the Divine Will is aligned with your goal, and if you've done things correctly (including preliminaries), it will manifest in due time.

The more you explore information and instructions about magick and using it to fulfill desires, the more you will notice a recurring theme: to actualize your desire, the emotions surrounding it must be exceptionally strong and passionate. Although this is true, there's a caveat: once you perform your magick ritual, this urge for a specific outcome must be let go. Since your desire and will was already sent out to the universe and higher realms, there's no point in having such anticipation in your mind anymore.

In essence, let go of any desperation for the result to come. There's no need to waste energy and time with that; just forget about it. If you don't, you're sending a signal that the magick you've performed is insufficient or incomplete.

Instead of filling your mind with anxiety and doubt, merely let go of the need to know how and when that particular out-come will reveal itself. Allow the outcome to manifest without forcing it into being. It must naturally come into your reality, and you need to give it enough energetic and mental space to actually manifest in your life. Maintain patience, perform magick, detach from the result, and let it come.

Magick can be done in different ways with the most varied methods. You can use planets, colors, elements, chakras, entities, spirits, objects, symbols, affirmations, visualizations, imagina-tion, etc. Exploring all of these options could last a lifetime. Therefore, for the sake of pragmatism and simplicity, we've chosen to employ powerful yet simple magick methodology that is easy to understand and apply, using a mixture of some techniques and systems, but without exploring others. Furthermore, as we progress in our magical path, we will know through intuition or external help where to proceed to deepen our magick experience.

Even though you will find magickal rituals and practices for divine purposes later in the book, the tools in this *Section 2* allow you to create your own. Of course, there is much more to learn and understand, but this knowledge will give you a solid foundation of self-experimentation and exploration. Don't be afraid to try things out, and always welcome magick into your life.

SECTION 3
The Practice

8

Deep Magick

In Deep Magick, we use magick to transcend the self. This is a topic scarcely explained in magickal lore. Transcending the self signifies going beyond our personality and individuality into a divine and impersonal form of existence, allowing us not only to become better versions of ourselves but to transcend our human boundaries. This is the real core and purpose of magick.

All students are free to adapt the rituals in this chapter to their own needs, or to use them as a guideline to create their own, as described in previous chapters. These rituals are aimed at transcending the self, the entity that you believe and feel that you are. We intend to go beyond the dichotomy of virtue/flaw or perfection/imperfection into the realm of divinity and Spirit. Previous success in the preconditions is imperative, as those practices and experiences will increase the likelihood of success in Deep Magick.

Before we leap into the practical aspect of Deep Magick, there's something each student of magick must grasp.

The Dimensions of Magick

We live in multiple dimensions. Some of them are obvious, such as the physical realm where our physical bodies operate, or the mental realm where our thoughts and imagination occur. There are countless more realms, but humans typically lack the conscious ability to access them. Mysticism, Occultism, and Magick possess methodologies that give us access to those subtler dimensions of Creation.

As some of these dimensions directly affect our physical, energetic, and mental world, we can create change in these subtler dimensions, which in turn affects our physical world.

Each tradition's system has its own distinct model, with its dogma, concepts, beliefs, and methods. Animal spirits, angels, saints, deities, divine names, elementals, gods, and even evil spirits are used as mediators between the magician and the subtler dimension he wants to reach or cause change. Despite all the differences between these systems and traditions, if you look closely, you will notice that despite contrasting labels, names, and significance, they are essentially talking about the same substance. Some practitioners get so caught up in their tradition that they fail to see that their system is only a way of attaining the same result.

Often, in magick, the universe is symbolized as the world tree, each branch with a "section" that carries a specific type of energy, an "intermediary" entity, color, planet, and so on. The branches stretch into the highest and purest divine worlds (sometimes representing divine virtues or quintessential qualities), while the roots of the tree dig deep into the densest and grossest subconscious dimensions (sometimes representing negative or impure qualities). This is a type of model of possible levels of consciousness.

We will delve into a magickal understanding of these dimensions, but instead of seeing them as multiple "worlds" or "divine spheres", we will view them as secular representations of levels of consciousness.

1 – Low Consciousness; The Inhuman Realm.

A step below human consciousness, where the mind lies in low awareness, incapable of reaching the human level of kindness, compassion, love, connection, or understanding. Such beings have yet to develop higher intellect and function through instinct, aggression, and by primal impulses of greed, lust, and darkness. What many call "Hell" or "Underworld". Though not a state typically found in human consciousness (but many nonphysical entities live with this type of consciousness), some humans do operate on this level, such as pathologically cold-blooded serial killers. This realm favors destruction.

2 – Ego Consciousness; Personal Realm; The practitioner state.

This dimension includes both waking consciousness and the subconscious. What many call "Earth" (not to be confused with the planet). It's a vast spectrum, and it can go from an incredibly selfish nature to a more compassionate one. Many entities function from this level.

As the practitioner of magick continues performing their practices and rituals, they will go from a lower grade of ego-consciousness to a more refined ego-consciousness. During this process, practitioners glimpse into the divine states of the next level.

3 – God Consciousness; Divine Realm; The magician state.

A superconscious state where the magician operates as a complete divine being in harmony with the universal mind. What many call "Heaven" or "Paradise". Though we may use magick to improve our lives in the personal realm, achieving the supreme magickal state on this level of consciousness is the ultimate purpose of magick. It's the Mystic's union with God.

As a practitioner of Deep Magick, the student must transcend from ego-consciousness into God-consciousness, thereby achieving both the impersonal dimension of the universal mind and the manifestation of perfection in the relative and personal realm of existence.

There are many levels between these, but they serve as a focal point on which the student can readily comprehend Deep Magick's purpose.

Magick to Transcend the Self

Magick to transcend the self requires a high degree of mental skills and mystical ripeness, putting it out of the realm of possibility for the vast majority of magick practitioners, who are mostly just seeking some change or improvement in their day-to-day self. However, we're well aware that the reader is not holding this book by chance.

All students have in themselves the possibility of achieving success in Deep Magick, if so they choose. We won't affirm that it will be smooth or quick, because it won't. There's no magic formula for immediate success here. Instead, it will require hard work, persistence, and an indomitable will to achieve magickal greatness.

The deeper the state of consciousness achieved, the more efficient and powerful magick will be. Magickal meditation prepares the mind and gets it concentrated, harmonizing, and aligning the energy body. The student must always strive to achieve a higher state of consciousness and relaxation before going into these magickal practices and rituals, as they facilitate the possibility of making more substantial magickal leaps. Another essential component is having an awakened third eye (inner vision), being aware of the vital force, and being able to use and manipulate energy. Therefore, do not disregard the preconditions.

The effects of these magickal rituals are unlikely to be instant. Powerful and enduring effects take more time to manifest. It also is highly contingent upon the practitioner's current magickal development and experience, karma, and competence on the preliminaries.

The following rituals predominantly use inner magick, mechanisms, and tools, instead of external aids and tools with a traditional outlook. The traditional ways are not irrelevant, but we've always followed a more self-sufficient nonpartisan approach, essentially through inner work, instead of dogmatic traditionalism and melodramatic rites. Some readers coming from a more classical background may find these magick rituals bizarre or senseless, but all that is required is an open mind and genuine motivation to perform them. There's a place for traditional ceremonial magick, but we will not address it in this volume.

We don't particularly appreciate when magick can't be done because a student doesn't have the required tools or the correct external environment. This doesn't signify that outward-oriented rituals and traditions don't work, but that tapping into the subtler dimensions directly with inner tools causes more substantial long-term positive effects in the psyche of the practitioners in regards to using magick to transcend the self.

The student should perform these magickal practices and rituals in the same physical place, which should only be used for magickal practice and nothing else. It is a *Magickal Laboratorium*, a space dedicated exclusively to magickal practice. It can be a whole infrastructure, such as a Temple, an entire division within a house, or a small space within a division. It is up to the student to choose according to their possibilities. Even a small space within their room, perhaps separated by a curtain, a screen (room divider), or something of a similar nature, is enough.

Deep Magick rituals are given in the proper order of execution. The practitioner can try any of them at any time, but they will work better if done in order. Some rituals require the completion of the previous ritual to be correctly practiced. They will not be successfully done in a couple of weeks, but this is magickal training of a lifetime.

All of these rituals can also be done in the inner Laboratorium/Temple, with the help of the inner Master, if you've connected with Him, as explained in the previous volume of *The Art of Occultism*. This will make the rituals more effective. You can also call or evoke any spirit or guides that you may be working with, as long as they are benign.

The times given are just estimates. If the instructions state to do something for 10 minutes, and the practitioner does it for 7 or 15 minutes, there will be no issues. With sufficient practice, the practitioner will get closer and closer to the correct time. There's no need to stress or disturb the mind with time-related preoccupations during the process.

Magick of the Subconscious Mind

The first step in Deep Magick is learning how to tap into and fully use the subconscious mind. This magick ritual works as the foundation for all magickal transcendence. The intention is to plunge the conscious mind into the subconscious, purify it, and establish a more permanent connection between both. Instead of being confined to trance, dream states, and so on, the subconscious mind becomes consciously accessible at all times in the background of wakefulness.

Procedure:

1. Enter into a higher state of consciousness using your preferred method.

2. Open the ritual by drawing a circle with your left hand's index finger. The left hand is symbolic of the subconscious mind. The circle must be done clockwise, starting at 9 o'clock. As you draw the circle in the air, you have to visualize that you are drawing it with a bright golden light, as if that light came from the top of your index finger. The size of the circle doesn't matter. This opening can be done with your eyes opened or closed. All Deep Magick rituals will use this opening.

3. With your eyes opened, look at the left hand (palm up). Your left hand represents the subconscious mind. Energetically charge it with the intention that it symbolizes the subconscious. You can do it by feeling the energy coming from your own being into the hand. There should be tingling, pressure, numbness, or a feeling of heaviness in your left hand. Do this to the best of your ability, for around five minutes or until you feel that it is sufficient.

4. Once step 3 is done, look at the right hand (palm up). Your right hand represents the conscious mind. Energetically charge it with the intention that it symbolizes the conscious mind. You can do it by feeling the energy coming from your own being into the hand. There should be tingling, pressure, numbness, or a feeling of heaviness in your right hand. Do this to the best of your ability, for around five minutes or until you feel that it is sufficient.

5. Once step 4 is done, put both hands facing each other and create a ball of energy in the space between them. Visualize it or use your imagination. Try your best to feel the ball of energy, as if there were pressure, warmth, or wind between your palms. This ball symbolizes the nexus between the conscious and the subconscious mind. Do it for around 5 minutes.

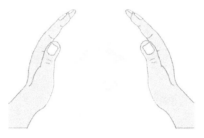

6. Slowly bring both hands together, feeling the pressure of the ball between them, until they clasp. This symbolizes the union of the conscious mind with the subconscious. Put that intention into this action.

7. Once they clasp (don't clasp them too hard), close your eyes, and feel them as one single unit, instead of two separate hands. Feel the warmth or the heat that they emanate towards each other.

8. When they feel like a single unit of energy, bring them into your chest, touching it with the back of your thumb, applying some light pressure.

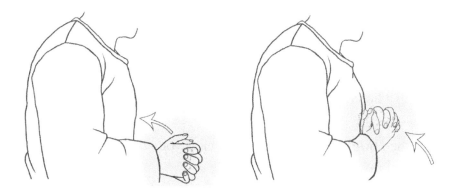

9. Feel a connection between your supraconscious mind (symbolically represented by both hands unified), and the heart. Take your time.

10. Drop the hands slightly.

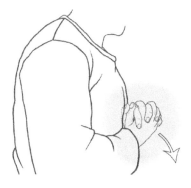

11. Bring the hands back towards the chest while taking a long inhalation. When they touch your chest, apply some light

pressure with the back of your thumb again, and hold the breath for 15 seconds.

12. Once the 15 seconds are over, slowly exhale while dropping the hands once again.

13. Repeat steps 10-11, ten to twenty times.

14. Once it is done, open your eyes, look at your hands, and with a fierce intention, mentally say: *My subconscious and conscious mind are one.*

See bright golden energy envelop your hands. Repeat this step 3 times.

15. Close your eyes, and quickly unclasp the hands.

16. Close the ritual by drawing a circle with your left hand's index finger anticlockwise, starting at 9 o'clock. As you draw the circle in the air, you have to visualize that you are drawing it with a bright golden light, as if it came from the top of your index finger. Make the size of the circle similar to the one you drew when opening the ritual. This closing can be done with your eyes opened or closed.

This magick ritual will require numerous attempts until you know it by heart. It will purify some hidden aspects of your subconscious mind that may be holding you back, and establish a more permanent and strong connection between the conscious mind and the subconscious. This is foundational work.

It should be practiced once per day for at least two months before proceeding into the next magick ritual.

When you deliberately open the doors of the subconscious mind, you begin to experience more creativity, energy, well-being, contentment, and wisdom. Even psychic abilities may manifest. The infinite intelligence of God greatly manifests through intuition and creativity in the subconscious mind. In humans, it lies mostly in potential, and for most people, it remains untapped throughout their lives.

The merging of the conscious mind and personal will with the subconscious also removes hidden inner obstacles that typically prevent practitioners from reaching deeper stages. Once the student's inner barriers are destroyed, all external barriers succumb as well. This is something that Deep Magick enables you to achieve.

Sacred Elemental Energy

The next step in Deep Magick is using elemental energies to plunge into the root of our psyche and cause multidimensional change and transcendence.

Due to the previous magick ritual, the student's conscious mind has dived deeply into the subconscious, enabling them to expand further and deeper into this richer layer of the mind. Some of these rituals may naturally develop powerful intuition, clairvoyance, clairaudience, visions, mind reading, etc., in some students. It's a natural and positive consequence.

In the subconscious realm, things don't function as rationally as on the conscious mind. The subconscious works more with visual imagery and symbols, and as we consciously delve further into it, we enter into subtle realms of ethereal imagery, archetypes, and powerful symbology.

Typically, the pentagram is used in magick as a way of representing the five elements. The five elements that a practitioner generally works with are: Earth, Water, Fire, Air, and Space. This last one can go by many different names, such as *Ether* (from Greek "the upper pure, bright air; firmament"), or *Akasha* (the Sanskrit word for the concept of "sky" or "open space"). The five elements are well-known in the world of magick, though there are also other elements.

They are not to be taken literally, but as a symbol, a token of energy, or a particular force. This understanding has been incorrectly interpreted by many, predominantly with the ascent of contemporary chemistry. Elements are not to be taken literally as if they were on the periodic table, but as magickal forces and archetypal energy to be used in practice. In magick, they are notably misunderstood.

Each of the elements is related to a specific type of purpose. Instead of reading an endless theoretical analysis about each one of them, you will learn how to put them into practice. The instructions in this book regarding elemental energy may be dissimilar to what you may have seen in other volumes. We prefer to adopt ease of understanding and pragmatic teachings, instead of dabbling with hypothetical charades that restrict the student to the plane of belief and impracticality.

Rather than working with "Spirits" or "Entities", you will use energy directly, mostly without intermediaries. However, you can invoke or connect with them or with your inner Master before each magick ritual, if you so desire. They can act as the vehicle of transmuting the your will into its direct manifestation, but it's not a requirement.

We will neither use the traditional alchemical symbols for the five elements, nor the common magick Pentagram. We will actually expand the five-pointed star into a six-pointed star, transforming a Pentagram into a Star of David, giving rise to a new "element" that requires each student's utmost attention. We'll disclose this 6th element in a later chapter.

You can select some of these rituals and perform them to awaken specific aspects of your multidimensional being, but they should be executed in their given order. Some rituals work on the always unavoidable purification, others on more advanced magickal aspects. Some effects and results will be more promptly noticed, while others will take a long time. It depends on the student's nature and karmic path.

Each magick ritual should be practiced for at least one month. Then, the student must take notes regarding its effect, and afterwards, try the next one. After six months of practice, the student must come back and repeat one or two rituals that they feel they need the most or those that brought the most substantial and positive changes. After choosing, the rituals must be practiced 2-3 times per week for six to twelve months to get their full effect. If that's too much time, the student can do each for three weeks only, instead of one month, but it won't be as powerful or efficient. Mystical states such as *Fire-Born Emptiness* will not be achieved with just a few weeks of attempts.

Duration: 3 weeks to 1 month for each magick ritual. To be practiced every day or, at least, every other day; then 6 to 12 months 2-3 times per week for the one or two that had the strongest effects.

EARTH
Magickal Equilibrium

The Earth element is the grossest and densest of all elements. Its energy works as a mechanism to balance and ground the student's mind and energy, and as a facilitator of manifesting or solidifying high-minded desires. A student may try to use it for mundane desires, but it will seldom work with such intentions. It works best if the goal is mystically or spiritually elevating.

Due to the nature of Deep Magick rituals, the student will engage and connect with completely distinct types of powerful energies. For that reason, energetic equilibrium and grounding must be integrated into the physical, energy, and mental bodies before advancing. A failure to achieve appropriate levels of energetic balance and grounding may result in less than adequate outcomes. This is the purpose of this magick ritual for those who are interested in advancing through Deep Magick.

Intention:
-   Achieving energetic equilibrium and grounding.

Procedure:

This ritual can be practiced barefoot in a natural setting, such as in a beach or park. If you want to practice it indoors, you need to first interact with nature's energy. Nature's energy is the perfect energy to achieve energetic equilibrium and grounding. Before initiating the ritual, go outdoors and look at a flower, touch a tree, or put your feet in the sand. Get to know the natural energy of Earth.

1. Enter into a higher state of consciousness using your pre-ferred method.

2. Open the ritual by drawing a circle with your left hand's index finger. The circle must be done clockwise, starting at 9 o'clock. As you draw the circle in the air, you have to visualize that you are drawing it with a bright golden light, as if that light came from the top of your index finger. The size of the circle doesn't matter. This opening can be done with your eyes opened or closed.

3. With your inner eye, visualize a white Star of David (six-pointed star). You must know to what point each element corresponds.

4. Bring your awareness to the bottom (Earth) of the Star of David.

5. As you continue to focus on that point, the whole star will gradually become green.

6. Once the star is green, switch your focus to the whole star.

7. As you focus on the green star, charge it with nature's energy. Visualize energy coming from nature, charging the star.

8. Bring the star to the Root Center at the bottom of the spine, and visualize roots coming out of the star, reaching far deep, below the surface, and tree branches growing upwards within your body.

9. All of nature's grounding energy is flowing through your body. Feel that energy filling up your body, energizing it, and balancing all of your energy centers. Do this for 10 to 15 minutes.

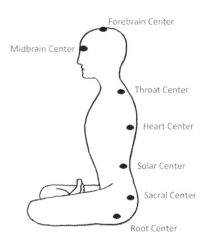

Forebrain Center

Midbrain Center

Throat Center

Heart Center

Solar Center

Sacral Center

Root Center

10. Feel your body and mind crystallizing, becoming like fertile soil for the manifestation of all magick goals and intentions.

11. Put your hands in your chest, or in the posture of prayer (such as when people say *namaste)*, and thank your inner Master if you've connected with or invoked Him, or show your gratitude to the grounding energy of Earth. Or you can use "Earth Guardians", "Earth Elementals" (also called "Gnomes" according to alchemical writings of Paracelsus), the archangel Uriel, the Universe, or any being, deity or entity related to the Earth element if you prefer. There's no problem with giving form to energy, if it helps the student. Thanking or showing gratitude can be done by mentally saying some words, or just by the intent and feeling of thankfulness, blessedness, and gratitude.

12. Close the ritual by drawing a circle with your left hand's index finger. The circle must be done anticlockwise, starting at 9 o'clock. As you draw the circle in the air, you have to visualize that you are drawing it with a bright golden light, as if it came from the top of your index finger. Make the size of the circle similar to the one you drew when opening the ritual. This closing can be done with your eyes opened or closed.

Whenever students feel imbalanced or out of touch with physical reality, or have dwelled for far too long in mystical states, they should practice this ritual. It will re-anchor their consciousness into their body and connect them with their primal energy centers and natural power.

It may look basic on the surface, but this type of magickal ritual is critical for magickal progress. Proper grounding must come from self-mastery of energy, but that requires years of diligent practice. Until that is achieved, magickal practitioners must resort to this ritual. Regardless of how high a student goes, their feet must stay put on the ground.

WATER

Magickal Purification and Healing

The element of Water can be used for constructive or life-giving principles, nourishing, healing, and purification, or to transform and transcend emotions. In this magick ritual, the It helps with gradual and progressive changes, deeply affecting all of the underlying aspects of the student's psyche and emotions. Water gradually purifies negative energy, heals psychological wounds, and helps to replace negative aspects with positive and constructive virtues.

Intention:
- Purification of the part of the subconscious mind that consists of repressed personality traits;
- Cleansing of flaws and blockages;
- Washing away negative karma;
- Healing psychological trauma;
- Transcending negative emotions;
- Purging anxiety, oppressive thinking, or any form of negativity.

Procedure:

Take a bath with warm water and salt before this magick ritual. It symbolizes purification, and it will help in this practice. As an alternative choice, you can go to the nearest beach and immerse yourself in the saltwater. Then you can do this practice on the beach if you so desire.

1. Enter into a higher state of consciousness using your pre-ferred method.

2. Open the ritual by drawing a circle with your left hand's index finger. The circle must be done clockwise, starting at 9 o'clock. As you draw the circle in the air, you have to visualize that you are drawing it with a bright golden light, as if that light came from the top of your index finger. The size of the circle doesn't matter. This opening can be done with your eyes opened or closed.

3. With your inner eye, visualize a white Star of David, and bring your awareness to the lower-left point (Water) of the six-pointed star.

4. As you continue to focus on that point, the whole star will gradually become blue.

5. Once the Star of David is entirely blue, switch your focus to the whole star.

6. Keep focusing on the Star of David, and visualize it com-ing above you.

7. Imagine bright purifying/healing "rain" coming out from the Star of David above, washing your body. Feel the water touching your head, arms, legs, and the whole body.

8. Start breathing very slowly. As you exhale, visualize all negativity, injuries, traumas, shadow aspects, flaws, blockages, negative karma, or the features that you decided to purify or get rid of (in order to heal or transcend), coming out as black smoke or liquid, and getting dissolved by rainwater.

9. What you get rid of may be nothing in specific. It may just be felt as an overall sense of letting go of all these weights and baggage that hamper your magickal path and life.

10. Once 10 to 20 minutes have passed, dissolve the Star of David, and take some more deep breaths. Then, put your hands in your chest, or in the posture of prayer (such as when people say *namaste*), and thank your inner Master if you've connected with or invoked Him, or show your gratitude to the

purifying and healing energy of Water. Or you can use "Water Guardians", "Water Elementals" (also called "Undines" according to alchemical writings of Paracelsus), the archangel Gabriel, or any being, deity or entity related to the Water element if you prefer. Thanking or showing gratitude can be done by mentally saying some words, or just by the intent and feeling of thankfulness, blessedness, and gratitude.

11. Close the ritual by drawing a circle with your left hand's index finger. The circle must be done anticlockwise, starting at 9 o'clock. As you draw the circle in the air, you have to visualize that you are drawing it with a bright golden light, as if it came from the top of your index finger. Make the size of the circle similar to the one you drew when opening the ritual. This closing can be done with your eyes opened or closed.

After performing this magick ritual for 2 to 4 weeks, if the student decides to advance to a more powerful version, they can practice the following unconventional yet effective ritual. It must be performed on an empty stomach.

1. Go to the bathroom, and get ready to take a shower. Bring salt.

2. Close the door and make sure you will not be disturbed in any way for the next ten to fifteen minutes.

3. Spread salt in the bathtub/shower cabin. Take off your clothes and get inside.

4. Enter into a higher state of consciousness using your preferred method.

5. Open the ritual by drawing a circle with your left hand's index finger clockwise, starting at 9 o'clock. As you draw the circle in the air, you have to visualize that you are drawing it with a bright golden light, as if it came from the top of your index finger. The size of the circle doesn't matter. This opening can be done with your eyes opened or closed.

6. Visualize the Star of David and bring your awareness to the lower-left point (Water element).

7. As you continue to focus on that point, the whole Star of David will gradually become blue. Once the star is entirely blue, switch your focus from the lower-left point to the whole star.

8. Keep focusing on the star, and visualize it coming above you, just like the previous ritual.

9. See bright purifying/healing "rain" coming out from the Star of David above, washing your body. Feel the water touching your head, arms, legs, and the whole body.

10. While the purifying/healing rain keeps pouring, take 10 to 20 deep breaths.

11. Turn on the cold water. You're going to take a cold shower for about 5 minutes.

12. As you begin to feel the cold water, your body will start shivering, and you will begin to take rapid breaths. It will be a

considerable shock. Even though you are already in a higher state of consciousness, your mind may become even more acute.

As the water falls on your body, every time you exhale, visualize all negativity, injuries, traumas, shadow aspects, flaws, blockages, negative karma, or the features that you decided to purify or get rid of (in order to heal or transcend), coming out as black smoke or liquid, and getting dissolved by both the cold physical water and the astral water coming from the Star of David.

What you get rid of may be nothing in specific. It may just be felt as an overall sense of letting go of all these weights and baggage that hamper your magickal path and life. Try your best to keep your focus.

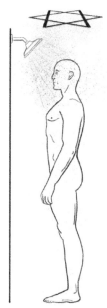

13. Once 5 minutes have passed, dissolve the Star of David, and take some more deep breaths. Then, turn off the shower.

14. Express your gratitude exactly like you did in the previous ritual (step 11).

15. Close the ritual by drawing a circle with your left hand's index finger anticlockwise, starting at 9 o'clock. As you draw the circle in the air, you have to visualize that you are drawing it with a bright golden light, as if it came from the top of your index finger. Make the size of the circle similar to the one you drew when opening the ritual. This closing can be done with your eyes opened or closed.

This deeper magick ritual is a much more powerful version, but it will not be as easy to accomplish as the first version. Coldwater is a potent catalyst for overall wellbeing, but it causes an enormous shock to the body and mind. Students with existing cardiovascular conditions should refrain from practicing this version.

If a student performs it once or twice a week for a year, countless physical, mental, and spiritual improvements will occur. It's an exceptionally powerful purifying and healing practice. It will change the student's life for the better.

FIRE

Fire-Born Emptiness

The Fire element is generally used as magickal energy when a student wants to work with practices related to the inner vision, passion, drive, or will. It also helps to cause a sudden and robust change, profoundly affecting the "surface" and visible aspects of the student's psyche.

However, in this magick ritual, we will use the element of Fire as destructive energy. While the element of Water progressively purifies a negative aspect, the Fire element destroys it.

Take the following example:

Imagine that you have a cup full of smelly, dirty water and that you want to get rid of that smell. If you purify the dirty water by removing contaminants, unwanted chemicals, solids, and gases, etc., you get clean water. Then, the problem of the bad smell has been solved, and that clean water can be used as drinkable water or to water the plants. That's how the element of Water in the previous magick ritual functions.

On the other hand, if you just get rid of the water completely, then the problem of the bad smell has also been solved. But you don't have water anymore, only an empty and dirty glass. If you wash that glass, you have a clean, empty glass, where new and different liquids can be poured. This is how the Fire element functions. It annihilates the negative aspects faster but without building or laying the foundations for the growth of the opposite positive features. Just like in the example, Fire leads to an empty glass (empty mind). This empty mind state, which is called *Fire-Born Emptiness* state, was induced by Fire "purification," though Fire purification is actually "destruction". The Fire-Born Emptiness state has beneficial qualities in itself, and can also be used as a portal or ground zero for higher achievements in later magickal rituals. The combination of both Water and Fire magick rituals give the best results.

Intention:
- Experience the flaming purification of the Fire element.
- Achieve the Fire-born Emptiness state.

Procedure:

Practitioners must never attempt to perform this magick ritual without an empty stomach.

1. Enter into a higher state of consciousness using your preferred method.

2. Open the ritual by drawing a circle with your left hand's index finger. The circle must be done clockwise, starting at 9 o'clock. As you draw the circle in the air, you have to visualize that you are drawing it with a bright golden light, as if that light came from the top of your index finger. The size of the circle doesn't matter. This opening can be done with your eyes opened or closed.

3. With your inner eye, visualize a white Star of David and bring your awareness to the lower-right point (Fire) of the six-pointed star.

4. As you continue to focus on that point, the whole star will gradually become red.

5. Once the star is red, switch your focus to the whole star.

6. Keep focusing on the star, and imagine it slowly transforming into an intense flame.

7. Once the star has completely transformed into a flame, see it coming into your body to engulf it. Your body will eventually be inside the flame, which burns intensively. Feel the heat.

8. Once you feel that your body is getting warmer, take a lengthy inhalation followed by a long exhalation, and then hold the breath for 20/30 seconds or for a count of 20/30. When performing the exhalation, you must contract the abdomen into the rib cage.

9. Repeat the previous motion at least 20 times, or if you want to push further, until you feel that an emptiness is spreading through your mind. You can use a string of prayer beads to help to count the breaths, such as a rosary or japamala.

Your body will get progressively hotter, and you may even begin sweating. Keep holding the image or feeling of being inside a burning flame the whole time. Once silence, tranquility, and emptiness consume you, stop the practice and inhabit that space. This is the Fire-Emptiness state.

10. When you feel that your body and mind have done enough and can't comfortably handle more Fire energy, take 10 to 20 slow breaths and dissolve the burning flame.

11. Put your hands in your chest or in the posture of prayer (such as when people say *namaste*), and thank your inner Master if you've connected with or invoked Him, or show your gratitude to the divine energy of Fire. You can use "Fire Guardians", "Fire Elementals" (also called "Salamanders" according to alchemical writings of Paracelsus), the archangel Michael, or any being, deity or entity related to the Fire element if you prefer. Thanking or showing gratitude can be done by mentally saying some words, or just by the intent and feeling of thankfulness, blessedness, and gratitude.

12. Close the ritual by drawing a circle with your left hand's index. The circle must be done anticlockwise, starting at 9 o'clock. As you draw the circle in the air, you have to visualize that you are drawing it with a bright golden light, as if it came from the top of your index finger. Make the size of the circle

similar to the one you drew when opening the ritual. This closing can be done with your eyes opened or closed.

If you didn't experience the Fire-born Emptiness state in the first few tries, you shouldn't despair. You must continue practicing this ritual because this sublime state is not easy to achieve without sufficient practice. Perhaps you must improve your ability on the preconditions or on the ritual *Magick of the Subconscious*. These are fundamental.

Repeated permanence in the Fire-Emptiness state is critical to going forward because it will be used in some of the more advanced magick rituals due to its ability to help consciousness expand its boundaries. The longer you manage to abide in this state, the better, and given substantial practice, deep inner peace and sparkles of joy will emerge. These feelings and peace will overflow into your life. New and fresh energy, focus, and vitality will ensue. Once a practitioner experiences these effects, they will look forward to practicing this magick ritual.

The final purpose of this ritual is to be able to trigger this state just with the mind. This is one of the powers of an advanced magick practitioner.

AIR

The Whisper of Wisdom

Air energy physically manifests as the common breath, and energetically, as the breath of life, also called prana, chi, vital force, pneuma, etc. The student of magick has extensively practiced with the Air element, even if unknowingly, through a multitude of practices and rituals, including in some of the preliminary practices. In this magick ritual, instead of using our vital force, we will access and use the subtlest form of the Air element: cosmic or universal vital force.

This magick ritual will allow the student to reach the universal unconscious layer of Creation. Beyond the personal subconsciousness lies the universal unconscious, where the collective mind dwells. This "mind" is not personal like an individual mind, but collective, being in some form or another present in all individual life forms. It has structures and processes which are shared and present in every one of us.

Through this universal unconscious substratum, all knowledge lies in potential/unmanifested. By tapping into this substrate, the student can access all types of wisdom, knowledge, or information. Albeit it is not in a tangible or objective form to be processed by the conscious mind (like reading words in a book), with the correct will, intention, and Magickal Seal, the student will be able to manifest this knowledge and information into their mental dimension and consciously access it through the five subtle senses.

This is achieved by the absorption and merging of the universal vital force (the subtlest form of Air) with the personal vital force (subtle form of Air) through the use of the Alchemical Seal of the Philosopher's Stone. This seal functions as the transmutational process by which we convert unmanifested raw information (base metals) into gold (actual wisdom and useful knowledge).

To successfully perform this magick ritual, the student must have achieved the Fire-Emptiness state of the previous ritual.

Intention:

- Obtain an answer to a question or request.

- Strengthen the connection between the universal mind and personal mind.

Procedure:

Ask yourself: "What do I want to know?" Your intention and will must be as clear and precise as possible.

What you want to obtain is an answer in the form of knowledge or information regarding something mystical, magickal, spiritual, or related to your current life, past lives, path, and so on. Don't use this magick ritual for egoic purposes, like trying to figure out what's the next best investment. It won't work. However, going with the investment example, if you've been thinking a lot about a specific investment, and feel that it is connected to your life's path and would like to know whether you should go for it or not, then it's acceptable to use this ritual for that.

The answer to your request may manifest through symbolic images in your mind's eye, sudden intuitive knowledge, silent words in your intellect, some event that happens minutes, hours, days, weeks, or months after you finish the practice, or in a multitude of different ways. Understanding divine signs is an art in itself, and it will be addressed in chapter 9.

1. Enter into a higher state of consciousness using a method related to Air energy (i.e., one that uses breath as the means of entering into a higher state of consciousness, such as Shamanic Breathing or the Mystic Breath from page 45/46.).

2. Open the ritual by drawing a circle with your left hand's index finger. The circle must be done clockwise, starting at 9 o'clock. As you draw the circle in the air, you have to visualize that you are drawing it with a bright golden light, as if that light came from the top of your index finger. The size of the circle doesn't matter. This opening can be done with your eyes opened or closed.

3. With your inner eye, visualize a white Star of David and bring your awareness to the upper-left point (Air) of the six-pointed star.

4. As you continue to focus on that point, the whole star will gradually become yellow.

5. Once the star is yellow, switch your focus to the entire star.

6. Bring the yellow Star of David into the middle of your brain.

7. Visualize universal vital force/energy coming from the universe into the yellow star, through the top of the head (i.e., the vital energy of the whole universe instead of the vital energy from your energy body). Do it for about 10 minutes.

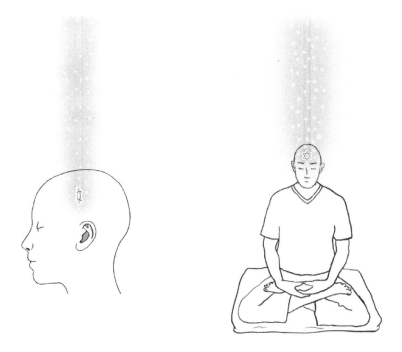

8. Once enough universal energy has been gathered, see your yellow six-pointed star slowly metamorphosing into the Alchemical Seal of the Philosopher's Stone (also known as the Hermetic Seal).

9. When the symbol of the Philosopher's Stone is visible with your inner eye in the middle of the brain, charge it with your will/intention. At this point, you don't have to keep the symbol visually present, but energetically present. You don't have to see it there, but you know it is definitely there through its energetic presence. Don't mentally repeat the question in your mind, but use the emotion and feeling associated with the yearning to know the answer as the source of the charging energy. Do this for about 10 to 20 minutes.

10. As soon as you finish charging it, let go of trying to maintain the seal, and trigger the Fire-Emptiness state with the power of your mind.

11. The answer or requested knowledge should emerge at any time in the Fire-emptiness state. However, it will still be unmanifested or unperceptive, or your mind will be incapable of translating it. Once that occurs, do your best to remain with that palpable yet untouchable energy.

12. Bring the Alchemical Seal of the Philosopher's Stone into your mind's eye again, and put step's 11 energy into it.

In due course, the seal will reveal or transform into the answer. This answer, information, knowledge, or wisdom, will manifest itself according to the Divine Will of your inner Master (Higher Self) or the universal mind of God. It probably will manifest during this magickal ritual, but if it does not, it means that for some reason, it can't happen now (you're not supposed to know at the moment) or that it will emerge later on.

13. Once it is finished, take 10 to 20 slow breaths, and dissolve the Philosopher's Stone seal. Put your hands in your chest or in the posture of prayer (such as when people say *namaste*), and thank your inner Master if you've connected with or invoked Him, or show your gratitude to the divine energy of Air. You can use "Air Guardians", "Air Elementals" (also called "Sylphs" according to alchemical writings of Paracelsus), the archangel Raphael, or any being, deity or entity related to the Air element if you prefer. Thanking or showing gratitude can be done by mentally saying some words, or just by the intent and feeling of thankfulness, blessedness, and gratitude.

14. Close the ritual by drawing a circle with your left hand's index finger. The circle must be done anticlockwise, starting at 9 o'clock. As you draw the circle in the air, you have to visualize that you are drawing it with a bright golden light, as if it came from the top of your index finger. Make the size of the circle similar to the one you drew when opening the ritual. This closing can be done with your eyes opened or closed.

The results for this practice may vary. For some practitioners, they will experience something mesmerizing in their first few tries. For others, it may take many more attempts. Frustration will block the successful completion, specifically taking into account the complex nature of this ritual.

This is dissimilar to accessing the conventional *akashic records* because instead of ejecting consciousness and trying to access the universal latent reservoirs of information, the practitioner is bringing specific information from the universal mind into their personal subconscious that then is converted into knowledge on their conscious mind.

For constant performers of this magick, universal wisdom will come up spontaneously regarding any subject at any time, even subjects that were not present in their conscious intention. It is truly magick.

SPACE

Voyage Into the Depths of Akasha

Akasha is not God or the *Primordial Substance*, as some mag-ickal works may lead the student to believe. It's an extremely subtle element, and it may be mistakenly seen as God because it shares some characteristics with God, namely, being infinite, undestroyable, and omnipresent. Space is everywhere, and there's no end to it.

However, despite being very subtle, it is a manifested form, unlike God, which is the underlying foundation or substance of all appearances, including those of a physical, energetic, mental, or causal nature, such as Space/Akasha.

In this magick ritual, the student will experience the primary characteristic of Space: its infinitude.

Intention:
- Experience infinity.
- Experience the boundlessness of Space.

Procedure:

1. Enter into a higher state of consciousness using your pre-ferred method. You may be sitting, standing, or lying down.

2. Open the ritual by drawing a circle with your left hand's index finger. The circle must be done clockwise, starting at 9 o'clock. As you draw the circle in the air, you have to visualize that you are drawing it with a bright golden light, as if that light came from the top of your index finger. The size of the

circle doesn't matter. This opening can be done with your eyes opened or closed.

3. With your inner eye, visualize a white Star of David and bring your awareness to the upper-right point (Space) of the six-pointed star.

4. As you continue to focus on that point, the whole star will gradually become violet.

5. Once the star is violet, switch your focus to the whole star.

6. As you continue to focus on the violet star, see it gradually dissolve until it becomes ethereal violet Space energy only. Then, absorb this energy.

7. After a few minutes, begin to breathe consciously, and with each inhalation, move the violet Space energy from the bottom of your body towards the top, and with each exhalation, move it from the top towards the bottom. Feel the sensation of the energy moving up and down.

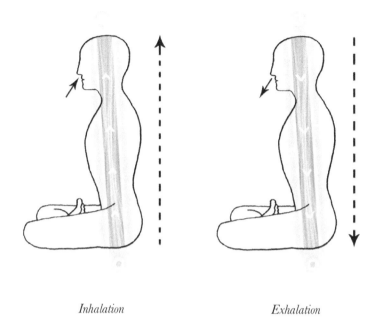

Inhalation   *Exhalation*

Perform this motion until your whole body is full of violet energy. It may take a while, but be patient. Do it for at least 15 minutes.

8. Continue to perform the same motion, but now do it faster and faster every time. Disengage the attention from the breath. Feel your astral body and awareness moving upward and downward with the movement of energy.

9. Do it so fast that the movement of energy is almost imperceptible. Gain some momentum, and when you feel ready, imagine that your consciousness is projected out of your physical body towards outer space.

10. You are now floating enveloped by the dark blanket of outer space. In the far distance, millions of cosmic lights shine

in your vast field of perception. Next to you, there's a beautiful blue pearl in this infinite expanse: planet Earth. Your physical body is there somewhere, quietly still.

11. Go back in time 5 billion years. You are so far back that the planet Earth does not yet exist. But, you're still there, in the dark blanket of space.

12. Try to find the beginning or end of space. Where is the beginning of space? Where is its end? Begin traveling at the speed of light, searching for them. Can you find where space starts or where it ends? Travel at the rate of one trillion times the speed of light. Search throughout the whole universe, looking for the beginning or end of space. Can anyone find them?

Space can't begin, and it can't end. Yesterday, today, or tomorrow, space is always the same: endless. At this moment, you realize that space is infinite. Space doesn't begin, and it doesn't end; it is present everywhere and at all times. Space is like God, the underlying foundation of all that is.

13. Begin to dissolve your astral body and merge with endless Space, with Akasha. Let yourself be only Akasha; let yourself experience the space of infinity and the infinity of space. Stay some time contemplating and experiencing the realization of infinity.

14. Once it is done, come back to your physical body, and move it slightly to make sure that your consciousness settles into it correctly. Then, take 10 to 20 slow breaths, and put your hands in your chest or in the posture of prayer (such as when people say *namaste*), and thank your inner Master if

you've connected with or invoked Him, or show your gratitude to the endless energy of Space/Akasha. You can use the Archangel Raziel, or any being, deity or entity related to Space/Akasha if you prefer. Thanking or showing gratitude can be done by mentally saying some words, or just by the intent and feeling of thankfulness, blessedness, and gratitude.

15. Close the ritual by drawing a circle with your left hand's index finger. The circle must be done anticlockwise, starting at 9 o'clock. As you draw the circle in the air, you have to visualize that you are drawing it with a bright golden light, as if it came from the top of your index finger. Make the size of the circle similar to the one you drew when opening the ritual. This closing can be done with your eyes opened or closed.

This is an intricate ritual that requires continuous attempts and practice, but the vast majority of students shall experience some degree of effect within a couple of weeks if they follow the instructions accurately.

Experiencing the infinity of Space is just like experiencing the infinity of God. Therefore, by experiencing the kernel of Akasha, the student is also experiencing a "quality" of God, even though God has no qualities. This is a taste of omnipresence and immortality.

<u>SPIRIT</u>

Magickal God-Force

The last element we'll address is *Spirit*. However, Spirit is not an element in itself, but the God-Consciousness that encompasses all the other five elements. Consequently, we can't use it as God-consciousness, but as the moving force of consciousness, which may be called Shakti, Divine Feminine, Mother, Holy Spirit, Goddess, etc., according to different traditions.

Here, we shall call it *Spirit's Breath* or *God-Force*. It is the most powerful energy, the primordial Force, the ultimate Creative Power. It's not some random force or power, but the supremely intelligent force and power behind the creation, design, sustenance, and eventually the end of the universe as we know it. The other five elements originate from Spirit, and it's where they shall ultimately return.

Through this magick ritual, practitioners will recognize that everything is one. In the previous magick ritual, they realized the endlessness of space and experienced the infinitude of God. In this ritual, they will realize the universal connectedness of everything.

Everything comes from the Primordial Substance, which is the underlying foundation or substance of all appearances. Everything that we call matter, energy, or thought has Spirit/God as its foundation. This foundation is inconceivable, unthinkable, and unknowable. It is the essential nature of all that exists.

Despite typically functioning as an individual being, the practitioner can erase their boundaries and experience cosmic unity. This is a life-changing experience, in a magnitude impossible to foresee. When a practitioner experiences the ultimate unity, they come back a changed being, with a cosmic perspective, instantly dropping the individual, limiting, and egoic point of view.

Those who achieve success in this practice are not students, but real magicians. Only mature magicians will successfully be able to conclude it.

This ritual is complex; it may require dozens, hundreds, or even thousands of attempts. It varies according to the practitioner's magickal readiness. It also requires the successful accomplishment of all of the previous rituals and preliminary practices. A student can attempt to practice it without having done the other rituals, but the effect won't be the same.

Intention:

- Lose body-awareness and the individual point of perception.
- Experience the rapture of God-Force/Spirit's Breath.
- Experience the universal connectedness of everything.

Procedure:

You need to perform this magick ritual near a place where you can comfortably lie down. Or you can bring a yoga mattress and place it near where you will perform the ritual.

1. Enter into a higher state of consciousness using your preferred method.

2. Open the ritual by drawing a circle with your left hand's index finger. The circle must be done clockwise, starting at 9 o'clock. As you draw the circle in the air, you have to visualize that you are drawing it with a bright golden light, as if that light came from the top of your index finger. The size of the circle doesn't matter. This opening can be done with your eyes opened or closed.

3. With your inner eye, visualize a white Star of David and bring your awareness to the top (Spirit) of the six-pointed star.

4. As you continue to focus on that point, the whole star will gradually become very bright.

5. Once the star is bright white, switch your focus to the whole star.

6. Begin chanting "Om" or "Aum" into the star, for 5 to 10 minutes. You can chant vocally, mentally, or both, but make sure the vibrations of your chanting go towards the star.

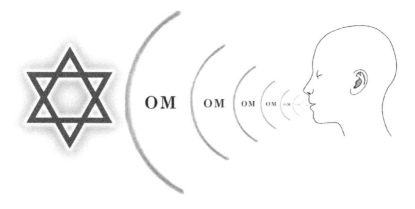

7. As you keep chanting, see the universal symbol of "Om" appearing in the middle of the bright white Star of David. This symbol represents the cosmic sound of Creation, and we will use it as a portal back to the beginning of Creation, particularly due to its imbued energy in the universal mind. It's symbolic of God-Force.

8. Lie down on your back in a comfortable position (on the mattress you brought, or on a sofa or bed).

9. Ask your inner Master or the representation that you have of God (it can be a bright sphere of energy or the void of formlessness if your predispositions give Him no form) to guide and help you expand your individual form into the universal form. This must be a genuine request. Be prepared and ready to let go of everything, and show with your intention and will that you are ready to experience this. Take your time, and let go.

10. Slowly turn your eyes upward as if they were looking at the brain. Vividly imagine that the bright white star with the Om in the middle is above your head, and is absorbing the perception of your body-awareness. Don't strain the eyes, and perform it smoothly. Do this for as long as you can, never less than 30 minutes.

Notice your body-awareness fading out. After some time, you can release the visualization of the six-pointed star and focus only on its presence in the space above your head. However, there's a strong possibility that the star will remain even though you are not actively visualizing it.

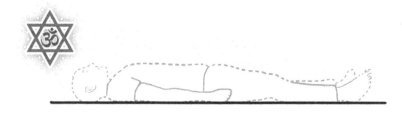

11. You will experience varied visions, hallucinations, and sensory experiences like floating, falling, etc. You may hear strange sounds or your name being called; dream imagery may begin to arise, trying to pull your mind into it. Disregard everything, and continue to perform the magick. Don't let sleep get the better of you. Keeping the eyes upward will impede you from triggering the sleep-reflex.

12. Once your body awareness has been greatly diminished (i.e., you can't feel most or all of your body, it is dormant, or it has fallen asleep), focus on Star of David with the Om, in the space above your head, and use all your ability to move your consciousness through its middle, precisely where the Om symbol is. See yourself piercing through it.

Going through the universal Om is symbolic of leaving your individuality behind, losing human boundaries, and experiencing universality and God. Be prepared to endure a colossal fear of dying. If you surpass it, you will experience the rapture of God-Force, which will lead you to the experience of the universal connectedness of everything. If you don't, there's always another try.

13. Once this magick is completed, if it was successful, show your gratitude towards God with the utmost sincerity you can express.

If it wasn't successful, ask God to reveal what's blocking your progress. Demonstrate that you are ready to go beyond your constraints and that you will tackle everything required to succeed in this ritual. Be thankful for the opportunity and show gratitude with the utmost sincerity you can express. You may not be ready, but it's merely a question of when as soon as you overcome what's blocking you. Showing gratitude towards God or the Primordial Substance can be done by mentally saying some words, or just by the intent and feeling of thankfulness, blessedness, and gratitude.

14. Afterwards, come back to your initial posture and finish off the ritual by drawing a circle with your left hand's index finger. The circle must be done anticlockwise, starting at 9 o'clock. As you draw the circle in the air, you have to visualize that you are drawing it with a bright golden light, as if it came from the top of your index finger. Make the size of the circle similar to the one you drew when opening the ritual. This closing can be done with your eyes opened or closed.

Losing the personal point of objective and subliminal perception into unity consciousness is a mind-altering experience for the magician. There are some accounts of it in some mystical and occult books, but there are no true words to describe the never-ending joy of being the whole: the Creator, Creation, and the Created. It's divine magick at its purest.

The Manifestation of God-Consciousness Magick

Through the successful completion of all of these magick rituals, a new and spontaneous modification will occur in the *Magickal God-Force* ritual.

This concluding magick ritual aims to temporarily transport the practitioner's consciousness from the personal realm into the inexhaustible experience of union with the whole of Creation. But with time and sufficient dedication, this unfolding will be reversed and transformed into an extinguishment of the practitioner's individual realm, giving rise to the full manifestation of the divine realm in their multidimensional being. This process can't be instructed or taught.

A magickal vacuum will emerge in the core of the magician, transforming their manifested existence into something no words or book can express. There's no state, symbol, affirmation, entities, energy, or anything that a student can perform to trigger it. It's just the natural breakthrough that takes place in a magician who is prepared to manifest the ultimate embodiment of God-consciousness.

Success in this ritual will not be granted to those who still have fantasies, hunger, or hopes of achieving something mundane, materialistic, or egoic, regardless of how small.

This progress towards a phenomenological eradication of multiplicity is proportional to the rise of the manifestation of the impersonal divine realm. The magician will, at last, be ready to dismantle their confined personal identity by embodying God-consciousness in human form—and there's no going back. This is the ultimate form of magick.

9

Divine Signs

Magick speaks to us subtly in the open, from the deepest parts of our soul, and from the very universe and life that we experience. It whispers to let us know we're on the right track, and shows us through life when we're going off course.

At first, most students miss all the signals. They perform magick, and they do get responses to their requests or indications that their magick is indeed working, but such signs typically go unnoticed. Understanding them is an art in itself, and the student has to be alert to everything, both within and without.

The ability to identify divine signs arises in those who are diligent and persistent with their practices. The mind rises to a higher level and acquires new sensitivity, enabling the student to read the language of magick, something that they couldn't do before, despite clues being in plain sight.

Students must be open to all types of signs because they can come from anywhere and anyone: a sentence read in a book, something a family member or a stranger says, the emergence of an unexpected memory, a song heard on the radio, a bird landing on the windowsill, the way the rain is falling, a silent inner voice, a graffiti on a wall, a dream, etc.

If you speak to magick, let it come in and listen to its message. It's not a question of looking for answers and seeing things where there are none, but of being observant of life and understanding its language.

10

Magickal Protection

Traditionally, in magickal rituals, a practitioner must do a circle of protection with salt, and then, use an athame or blade to banish negative spirits/energy in each of the four cardinal directions. This circle can only be released when the magickal ritual finishes.

Magickal Protection is critical when a practitioner is interacting with negative or highly dubious entities, or practicing dark types of magick. Performing non-benevolent types of magick can push the student's mind into that very same state, and one may suffer the consequences of that parasitical energy.

If the practitioner has benign and positive intentions, if they only interact with benevolent beings, or if they have connected with their inner Master as instructed in *The Art of Occultism*, then they don't have to worry about protection.

Nonetheless, as the reader may have noticed, each ritual in Deep Magick is opened with an astral circle. Unlike a circle with physical limitations (e.g., one that is done with salt), this astral circle is all-encompassing. This means that the student is safeguarded in all areas and dimensions because the circle is done mentally with the mind, energy, and feeling.

The astral circle has an inherent protective energy because it has been universally imbued in the collective mind that it serves that purpose. Therefore, the practitioner doesn't have to infuse it with a protective intention.

However, there's a place for a different kind of protection: outside of magick rituals.

Inevitably, during our everyday life, we regularly engage with all types of energy from people, places, objects, etc. Whenever there's energetic interaction, unless we already have some mystical development (acquired through the practice of mysticism, occultism, magick, or spirituality), which shields us from such energies, our energetic system will absorb some of that energy and emotions, even if we are unaware of them, just like people unavoidably breath air pollution in a city such as Delhi.

Typically, the more advanced a student is, the stronger their emotional maturity and energetic field are, and therefore, the less they are affected by others' thoughts, energy, and emotions. Nonetheless, every student is susceptible to energetic influence, regardless of their degree of development. This influence, when negative, functions as pollution that can enter into their system and alter their state of mind, thereby knocking down their elevated level of thinking, feeling, and acting. It affects their mind and state of being.

Here's how each student can impede this from occurring:

Intention: Protection from external negative energies.

Procedure:

1. Enter into a higher state of consciousness using your preferred method.

2. Open the ritual by drawing a circle with your left hand's index finger clockwise, starting at 9 o'clock. As you draw the circle in the air, you have to visualize that you are drawing it with a bright golden light, as if it came from the top of your index finger. The size of the circle doesn't matter. This opening can be done with your eyes opened or closed.

3. With your inner eye, visualize a bubble made of golden light originating from your Heart Center, which grows and ends up enveloping your body.

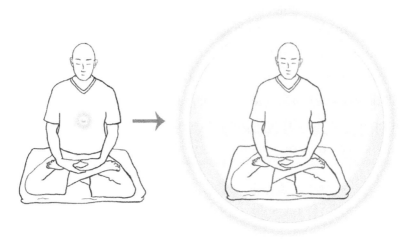

4. Affirm vocally or mentally, with confidence and certainty: *This bubble of energy is an indestructible shield. No negative energy can penetrate it.*

5. See the bubble's golden light becoming so dense that it is impossible to see from outside what's inside, and vice versa.

6. Close the ritual by drawing a circle with your left hand's index finger anticlockwise, starting at 9 o'clock. As you draw the circle in the air, you have to visualize that you are drawing it with a bright golden light, as if it came from the top of your index finger. Make the size of the circle similar to the one you drew when opening the ritual. This closing can be done with your eyes opened or closed.

After achieving a higher state of consciousness, steps 2 to 5 shouldn't take more than five minutes.

This magick ritual must be performed every day for 30 days, preferably in the morning after waking up. Then, it can be done only once per month.

The bubble's energy may become so strong that you not only feel it as a tangible presence or "warmness in the air", but other sensitive beings may feel it as well.

You can also use it as a method of protecting people, objects, or places, by using the same energy to create an energetic bubble around them. An important caveat is that the magick ritual will need to be done at least once per week to maintain its effect (after the initial 30-day period), unless the object, person, or place develops a magickal energy of its own.

This occurs because a practitioner grows and develops their magickal ability, and therefore, their natural levels of protection and magickal presence also increase. On the other hand, unless the person being protected is also developing their own magickal ability, their magickal shield will require constant maintenance.

A further observation is that one's ability to protect others (or other things) depends on one's magickal and mystical advancement, and on the karma of the person.

Ultimately, you must know that you can't perform magickal protection to shield yourself from your path or life. Life is meant to be lived, felt, experienced, and transcended. Obstacles and problems will appear, but with enough will and dedication, you shall overcome them.

11

Obstacles to a Successful Magickal Practice

uring magickal practice and rituals, many obstacles will arise. Knowing beforehand which barriers students are more likely to face, will prevent them from getting stuck or stagnated.

Some of these obstacles will certainly arise. The purpose is not to avoid them, but to transcend them and keep moving forward. Here are some of the most common ones:

- Not approaching the study and practice of magick with steadfastness, commitment, and diligence.

- Losing concentration or being distracted during the practice or ritual.
- Lack of real desire or intention.
- Being in a poor state of mind before the practice or ritual.
- Being afraid of change or of not being able to handle what will ensue.
- Lack of self-confidence or self-esteem.
- Being impatient or expecting an instantaneous change.

Notwithstanding these obstacles, the biggest one in magick is *doubt*.

Doubt

All students experience doubt when they begin working with magick. It is a part of the magickal process.

These doubts may manifest in a myriad of ways, for example, a student might feel like they aren't certain whether they are performing the magick correctly or if it will work; they may question whether they are worthy, or have a general feeling that they will fail. They may also experience a hazy sensation of uncertainty or thoughts of screwing things over.

These types of thoughts, feelings, and doubts are habitual at first. Students shouldn't worry too much about them. Most people do experience some doubt when they attempt to do something new. In unconventional subjects, such as magick or spirituality, this is notably true. But no one should let doubt handicap them. Little by little, the student will make progress and gain confidence. It's just a matter of sufficient practice and knowledge until doubts fall away.

Magick is not dead or insentient; it has a life of its own. If students approach it with honesty and truthfulness, and work through their doubts, they will be rewarded with positive outcomes beyond their expectations.

Fear

Fear is another big opponent in magick. Students may experience dozens of different fears, but some are more common than others:

Fear of Becoming Crazy or Psychotic

This is a widespread fear in Magick, Mysticism, and Occultism, and not without reason, considering that practitioners are altering their state of consciousness, accessing the subconscious, heightening their mental abilities, upgrading their psyche, changing their physiology, etc. Is there a legitimate motive for this fear?

If a student is a mentally healthy individual, follows the instructions as written and doesn't request the presence of, or attempts to interact and connect with malicious entities, then that fear has no grounds. Moreover, all students must remember that they have protection and that nothing can penetrate it. Malicious entities can only harm you if you leave your protection or consent to break it.

If a student's mind is completely unstable or unhealthy, they shouldn't be doing magick, but working on getting it back to normal levels through correct therapy and standard meditation.

If a student doesn't follow the instructions correctly, what may happen is that nothing happens.

If a student actively pursuits engagement and interaction with malevolent entities, and breaks the circle of protection, then such a student is inviting some dark and weird occurrences.

Nonetheless, the practice of magick will not make you insane. Instead, it will open the door to the subtle realm of Creation, illuminating and expanding your mind. You will be more conscious and sagacious than before your magickal journey.

Making a connection with your inner Master is another foolproof method of disabling the possibility of something bad occurring. That's why this book, *The Art of Magick*, comes third in the collection, after *The Art of Mysticism* and *The Art of Occultism*. Even if it can be read as a single book, it is best if you've read the other two *a priori*, particularly concerning the subject of union with the inner Master.

Fear of Ridicule or Humiliation

Students of magick may fear that if someone finds out that they're performing magick, they will be ridiculed or humiliated.

First and foremost, students must always do their practice and rituals in a place or room where they can never be disturbed. If you live with someone that doesn't know that you're performing magick, there's a chance that they will sooner or later end up hearing you speak alone in a closed room. In that case, you have three choices:

- Be honest and tell or explain to them what you're doing. They may understand and even join you. If they try to ridicule you, the question is: what are you doing by living with such a person? Your values and priorities are very different;

- Perform your magick when you're home alone or in nature where nobody is present;

- Ignore or don't care what others think.

You may feel that society is secretly judging you for what you're doing: "Are you insane? You're doing Dark Ages absurd practices!"

This is an obstacle present in the collective unconscious of mankind, but it can be transcended. The practice of Mysticism, Occultism, or meditation will certainly help you overcome this issue because the higher degree of consciousness and alertness acquired through practice makes your mind unaffected by such comments, remarks, or even energy.

Fear of God

Students with a religious background may feel like what they're doing is wrong, evil, or sinful, and that God will punish them. This is entirely false and a limited, dogmatic view.

If you have this fear, notice how you are anthropomorphizing God and, therefore, giving Him human characteristics, limiting Him, and limiting yourself.

The reason you are reading this work or entering into a magickal path is because you want to transcend your current limitations and achieve more both as a human and as a divine being. You are embarking in the path of magick to erase those very conditionings and blockages that linger around your psyche.

Fear of Karmic Repercussions

If a student's magick does not harm anyone, why would they fear karmic repercussions? If it does harm someone, why is the student doing it? Nobody improves by hurting or damaging others, but by transcending their own limitations into a higher ground of understanding and knowledge. If a student uses magick as a way to self-improve, self-develop, or self-transcend, it is evident that such transformation will also help others, directly or indirectly. There are indeed karmic repercussions to that, but they are good ones.

Fear of Not Being Protected

If a student follows the protection instructions, then this fear is unfounded. The circle of protection is impossible to break, and the only way a practitioner becomes unprotected is if they leave it or if they consent to break it. There is no other way. Additionally, if a student only interacts and engages with positive energies and entities, what is there to be fearful of?

Fear of a Paranormal Experience

This is a rather irrational fear. Most students crave for a paranormal experience: a peek into the divine, the feeling of total rapture, the hearing of the voice of an entity, a drop in temperature in the room, the quick unclouding of clouds to reveal a presence or message, an out-of-body experience, an object moving without anyone touching it, a sudden increase in awareness that unveils otherworldly visions or lights, etc. However, if any magickal experience actually occurs, students get scared.

Imagine the occurrence of a complete materialization. Most students would have a heart attack. Wanting something "supernatural" to occur, but inwardly being scared that it happens, is something that all practitioners of magick have experienced. What occurs is a mixture of excitement, wonderment, shock, adrenaline rush, dopamine release, and fear of the unknown.

Oftentimes, after a ritual, strange things may happen. You may hear weird noises, feel strange sensations, glimpse surreal colors, smell out-of-this-world aromas, or even have completely uncharacteristic thoughts. This is normal and nothing to be scared of. Magick bridges the ordinary and extraordinary worlds together, thinning the boundaries of gross and subtle dimensions.

Given sufficient practice, what appears to be out of this world will be commonplace and become the new normal. If anything truly negative is about to occur, and your fears are about to materialize, remember that you do have protection activated, so nothing can happen to you. Furthermore, if you have connected with your inner Master, then you truly have nothing to fear; the inner Master is the light that dissolves all darkness.

SECTION 4
The Musing

12

Black Magick vs. White Magick

In magick, some sects are firm proponents of what they call "black magick", while others are entirely against it. But which one is right?

Students of magick must understand that viewing magick as black or white is an inherently wrong perspective. Our lives are not monochromatic, but full of several intermixed colors, and magick is no different.

We live in a dualistic reality. There is no black without white, left without right, high without low, above without below, distant without near, beginning without end, beauty without ugliness, sweet without bitter, silence without noise, positive without negative, here without there, joy without sorrow, success without failure, or life without death. There is always an opposite because everything has its counterpart. They are distinct grades of the same endless spectrum.

It is widely assumed that if a magician performs "white magick", they are doing a good deed. Examples of this would be to connect with a divine entity or doing a ritual to help heal a sick person.

On the contrary, it is believed that if a magician performs "black magick", they are doing an evil deed. Examples of this would be to cause senseless injury to people or attempting to kill someone.

In magick, most acts lie in the middle of the spectrum: not entirely white, not entirely black. If a burglar entered into your house at night and had a gun pointed at your family, and you had the choice to end that burglar's life, saving your family, would you do it? Would that be considered black magick or not, conceding that you're saving your family's life?

If you had a family to feed, and your company's wealthy CEO had unreasonably fired you with no warning, and without providing severance pay, merely because of a comment you made regarding his beloved football team, would it be considered black magick if you did some ritual to attempt to gain compensation from his company? Some people would say that you are using magick to attack a company and someone out of revenge, and that you should use magick to help you find a new job instead. Others would say it's entirely fair.

What we wish to demonstrate is that there's no such thing

as exclusively black or white magick. Most acts of magick are "grey". It always depends on the outlook of the practitioner performing the magick. While for some, an act of magick is considered white magick (saving your family), for others, it may be black magick (ending someone's life). It's always contingent on the student's discernment, conscience, and soul.

However, students must realize that anytime they perform magick, they are interacting and immersing themselves with that energy. So, if a student attempts to perform or engage in practices that deal with negative energy (energy that has a dissonant frequency) or with wicked intentions, they are bringing that energy into their own being, absorbing some of it in the process. It's like setting yourself in flames to burn someone down. The relief you think you may get by doing it will be overshadowed by the suffering that it will bring.

Magick is like a tool. It can never be good or bad, black or white. It is what magicians make of it, what we make of it. It's up to the student to decide where their intentions lie: if in clouded shadowy practices, or in the realm of divinity, of God Himself.

13

The Magician

agick is the means to acquire the perfect equilibrium, bringing to completion our desire for two apparent paradoxical matters: self-transcendence and personal fulfillment. But this cannot be achieved by treating it as a hobby, or with an insincere and trivial attitude. It demands true dedication to our personal journey, maturity to face inevitable adversity, discipline to keep going forward even when it seems like it's not working, and responsibility for our actions and intentions.

To reach this level of compromise and intensity, the student must arrive at a point where they realize that what the common world currently provides is not enough. Then they will look for higher forms of knowledge, understanding, and pleasure, beyond what family, friends, university teachers, figures of authority, and contemporary science propose. Magick provides precisely that, if approached and used correctly. It awakens a fountain of unlimited power in the student.

However, magick also has its pitfalls. In mystical circles, there's often a widespread attitude where authentic magicians, spiritual saints, yogic siddhas, bodhisattvas, mystics, and adepts of occult arts, are granted a colossal magnitude of ritualized adoration and veneration. That's comprehensible considering that they represent what all students of magick ultimately seek.

The prevalent concern arises when such people are stereotyped, made larger than life, and attributed all kinds of virtues and qualities that rare human beings can ever match up to. This gives the impression that such a state is impossible to reach, and it can negatively impregnate the subconscious of a new or intermediate practitioner with such beliefs.

We may expect the magician, mystic, or high occultist to be some exceptionally holy personage that even the wind wouldn't dare to blow when they walk outside. But this is not the case. Magicians are divine because they've dedicated their lives to the art of magick; they've put in years of effort and relentless determination, and have improved and transcended their self. They are the living epitome of magick. But they are also human beings.

All students of magick can also become magicians. It doesn't matter if they have weak self-discipline, or can't seem to meditate or perform rituals correctly. Perfection comes with practice. With dedication and discipline, the core of magick becomes your center, and as a magician, you will realize your purpose in the ever-continuous act of the divine creation that this universe truly is. Then you are also the embodiment of magick in human form.

14

The Ultimate Teaching of Magick

Many beginners believe that after a couple of weeks of magickal practice, all of their problems will evaporate. This is a mistaken view. Magick won't solve all of their dilemmas, but it will give them power, confidence, and wisdom to face all of life's multidimensional layers. Magick will help you change your circumstances, but only as far as you allow yourself to change.

Advanced students of magick may experience their fair share of incredible events and supernatural occurrences; their life may change for the better, and their identity may acquire new virtues and insights that were previously untapped within their subconsciousness. But after some time of living like this, their mind will become normalized to these occurrences. Miracles stop seeming like miracles and more like regular events; life goes on, and new challenges find their way in; intuition begins to seem obvious and incapable of solving deeper mysteries and decoding the universal DNA of God. Magick emancipated them from their usual way of living, but it trapped them into a subtler dimension.

At this point, students must let go of their usual way of approaching magick to be able to comprehend the ultimate magickal axiom: *as long as someone attempts to use magick, they are separated from it.*

If a student is separated from it, they aren't allowing the full potential of magick to manifest; they are creating a limiting dualism between themselves and magick. It's only when this dichotomy ends, when the magician is one with magick, that magick is realized to be the driving force of the universe.

We are that driving force. We, magicians, are magick. We don't use it; it is us. This is the ultimate secret that magick will teach you.

Epilogue

Today, almost all human beings are unable to be free from the constraints imposed by their own self-limiting beliefs. They suffer from the malady of having an unpurposeful and meaningless existence.

Readers who commit themselves to magick will recognize that it is not a fool's errand.

Magick can be a powerful tool that fundamentally changes the direction of our lives. It gives us the ability to transform, improve, and transcend. It is an investigative path, a journey of seekers that yearn to penetrate the surface of reality and directly experience what lies underneath.

It is up to each reader to show how sincere their dedication to magick is. We hope that this work motivates you to go far into Deep Magick, and achieve magickal and spiritual success.

Want to read more books like this? Show your feedback with a sincere review, or send an email to the author at mysticsarom@gmail.com, telling him what you thought about the book and what you'd like to see in new books (more mystic, occult and spiritual content, sharing more knowledge regarding practices, divine abilities, metaphysical explorations, etc.).

www.sacredmystery.org

Publications

The Art of Mysticism

Practical Guide to Mysticism & Spiritual Meditations

The Art of Occultism

The Secrets of High Occultism & Inner Exploration

The Art of Alchemy

Inner Alchemy & the Revelation of the Philosopher's Stone

Subscribe to Gabriyell Sarom's Newsletter and receive the book:

Divine Abilities: 3 Techniques to Awaken Divine Abilities

www.sacredmystery.org

Made in the USA
Las Vegas, NV
27 July 2024

93031736R00090